Children at Play
learning gender in the early years

Children at Play
learning gender in the early years

Barbara Martin

Trentham Books

Stoke on Trent, UK and Sterling, USA

Trentham Books Limited
Westview House   22883 Quicksilver Drive
734 London Road   Sterling
Oakhill   VA 20166-2012
Stoke on Trent   USA
Staffordshire
England ST4 5NP

First published 2011

British Library Cataloguing-in-Publication Data
A catalogue record for this book is available from the
British Library

ISBN 978-1-85856-484-5

Designed and typeset by Trentham Books Ltd, Chester and printed in
Great Britain by 4edge Limited, Hockley

Contents

Acknowledgements

I would particularly like to thank all the staff and children at 'Ash Vale' School who gave their time and made me so welcome. I feel enormous appreciation and respect for the children who generously shared their ideas and life in school with me. I learned so much from them and without them there would be no book. In many ways this is their book, and I dedicate it to them and to all young children in early years classes. Thanks to Lan and Ravi for their wonderful drawings for the cover of the book.

Many thanks to my PhD supervisors Rosalyn George and Carrie Paechter for their professional and personal support, for their wisdom, encouragement and inspiration. Additional thanks to Carrie Paechter for encouraging me to write this book and for writing the Foreword. Thanks to Rachel Fletcher and RF Design for their professional help with the diagrams. Thanks to Gillian Klein at Trentham for guiding me so kindly and expertly through the process of publishing the book.

Thanks to my father Keith and to my sister Pam for their sustained interest and support for my work over the years. Thanks to Katie, Lilly, Tanis, Marian, Mona, Sheila, and Shirley for their encouragement and helpful comments. Last, but not least, a big thank you to my partner Helen for her endless patience, enthusiastic discussion of ideas and practical help throughout my research and during the writing of this book.

Foreword

I t is a great privilege to be asked to write a Foreword to Barbara Martin's excellent book. I am really pleased to be introducing a work of such interest and importance.

It is well established that the early years of schooling are a period of enormous significance for young children, both socially and educationally. It is at this time that children lay important foundations for not just their education as a whole but also for their identities in relation to the groups of which they are a part. Going to nursery and subsequently into primary schooling is the first time many children are expected to operate in the world as individuals, without the support of their families. They have to learn to operate as part of the community of the nursery and of the school, and to understand what it means to be a nursery and then a schoolchild. As part of this, children learn what it is to be a boy or a girl in such a community. It is this process that Barbara Martin analyses with such care and insight.

The central importance of this book lies in the opening up of specific communities of practice of masculinity and femininity: those found in Ash Vale nursery and reception classes. Martin's detailed observations demonstrate how the children arriving at nursery observe the behaviour of those already established there and try to emulate it. She shows how new children are supported by others to become legitimate peripheral participants in nursery and then reception activities, how 'correct' behaviour is modelled and 'incorrect' behaviour censured. Martin's careful uncovering of these processes allows us to see how forms of masculinity and femininity are constructed between children in the two settings, and how they develop and evolve, both for the individual and for the group, as children move through the spaces and times of nursery and reception life.

A key finding of the research described in this book is that an individual child's developing understanding of what is 'permissible' for their gender is progressively limited by the group of children as a whole, during the first few weeks of school. As Martin points out, children of this age are keen to demonstrate that they understand to which gender category they themselves belong. They do this by behaving in ways that reflect their understanding of what being a member of that category means. First, however, they have to work out what it is to 'be a boy' or 'be a girl' within the nursery setting. They observe the play of older, more established, children, and take note of when their own behaviour is remarked upon, praised, or censured, by others. Children remind each other, both directly and by example, that pink is for girls, not for boys, that only bigger boys get to play football, and that skipping is something that all girls can (eventually) do but boys will never learn.

As Martin demonstrates, much of this 'gender learning' takes place through exclusion, particularly of girls, but also of younger and lower-status boys, from specific spaces in the nursery. As has been observed in many studies, much of the classroom and playground space is dominated by boys, who co-operate to exclude girls from anywhere they themselves want to be. Although this is resisted by girls – and Martin describes one incident in which girls banded together to take over the usually male-dominated climbing frame – much of the time these exclusionary practices allow boys to prevent girls from gaining access to certain forms of learning, particularly those which involve gross motor movement or masculine-labelled objects such as toy cars or construction materials. At the same time, local child 'rules' about what counts as masculinity prevent boys from participating in other forms, such as caring role play.

The detailed evidence about children's play in this book is fascinating in itself. Through Martin's lucid and readable account, we gain crucial insights into the world of the children: how they see each other, how they understand gender, how they enact their identities. There are very few studies of this kind already published, and even fewer from the UK, so this alone would make it a welcome addition to the literature. It is particularly important because of the age of the children: we see them negotiating their identities with others and with themselves, as they move through the crucial processes of starting Reception and then starting school. We also see how apparently innocent and sensible induction practices for new children starting school themselves act to reinforce gendered behaviour. The longitudinal aspect of this study allows us to follow how children change as they progress from one form of education to the next. We can see, for example, how children who were previously moving freely around the nursery learn to keep their bodies in check to perform the role of schoolchild.

Martin provides a strong critique of 'developmentally appropriate practice' and its effects on early years provision. She argues, following Walkerdine and Lloyd and Duveen, that such approaches allow teachers to ignore gendered behaviour and to treat as 'natural' particular constructions of masculinity and femininity. In particular, they permit boys' domination of classroom and play-ground spaces to go unchallenged and prevent teachers from addressing children's conservative approaches to gender.

Barbara Martin's analysis of how boys and girls construct masculinities and femininities through play, and the messages from this for early years edu-cators, are vitally important. The clarity of Martin's writing makes these messages crystal clear. It is essential that we heed what she is saying. The early years of schooling are a crucial period for the development of children's ideas about what it is to be boys and girls. We cannot let the children alone decide what is permitted to one gender or the other: this reduces the scope and the learning of both boys and girls. We need to intervene in how children police gender in the early years. By doing so we can help both boys and girls to develop more flexible ideas about themselves, and thereby have access to wider educational and life opportunities. A good place to start is by reading this book.

Carrie Paechter
Professor of Education
Goldsmiths, University of London
May 2011

Introduction
Playtime

Gender dualism

I t is a typical Tuesday morning in Reception class. The children are in their first term in Reception. The teacher, Ms Foster, has told the children they can choose from the activities she has set up in the classroom. She is busy with a Literacy group, and the classroom assistant, Ms Kent, is reading books with individual children. I go and sit by the construction area, which is set up with playdough on one table and wooden bricks on the carpet. Two boys, Tu and Ryan go immediately to the construction area. A girl, Ayan, goes to sit at the playdough table.

Tu making gun with wooden bricks by himself.

Tu:'Pu, pu' (points gun out of entrance).

Ryan sees, comes to join him. Gets two bricks and points them like a gun.

Ryan to Tu: 'I got a shotgun!'

Tu: 'We pretend we got shot.'

Tu: (urgently to Ryan) 'The monster still coming! (repeats several times, both boys crouching down at entrance to construction area, pointing guns, and firing them at 'monster' outside, out of sight.)

Ryan: 'I got him!' (has advanced out of the construction area to fire shots in open.)

Daniel comes and sits at playdough table next to Ayan.

Ryan turns his gun and points it at Daniel.

Daniel sees him, gets up and joins in the gunplay.

Daniel gets a long brick: 'This is my gun. I'm the leader.'

Three boys crouch in corner together, very close, guns pointing to 'invisible enemy'.

A girl, Jala, comes in, sits on floor by tray of bricks, begins to build a tower. The boys are taking up all the space in the area and Jala stays only a few minutes. Tu kicks down her tower as soon as she leaves.

Ryan: 'The baddies are out there. They don't know we're here!'

Tu: (in entrance, jumping up and kicking out, very excited) 'I got weapons I gonna kick him in the botty and he dead now. The monster dead!'

Tu: 'I pick a piece up, I break it! Ryan! Ryan!'

Ryan (loudly, excited): 'Look at my gun Daniel! I got two guns!'

A girl, Ayan, has been quietly making small balls at playdough table.

Ayan goes over to Tu: 'Tu, look! I made too much balls!'

Tu: (contemptuously): 'No, I don't want dat. I want to play with Ryan!'

Ayan goes back to playdough table.

A girl, Ellie, comes in, sits down and starts taking bricks from the tray.

Ellie starts giving bricks to Tu, and he puts them into a small drawstring bag.

Tu: 'I got lots I can buy something.'

Ellie starts arranging small cubes along the long brick that Daniel used earlier as a gun.

Daniel to Ellie (loudly): 'That's my *gun!*' (reaches over and takes the brick from Ellie).

Ellie looks upset and immediately leaves the area.

A boy, Jake, comes in, picks up bricks and points them like a gun.

Ryan to Jake: 'That's not a gun! You have to have one like this!' (holds out his brick to Jake).

Jake (excited): 'No, look, I got a machine gun.'

Jake: 'I can make a circle. I got a door shape.'

(I am surprised by this sudden change of topic, but then see that Ms Foster has come into the area. The talk is about circles and squares, until she goes out).

Here we see four boys enjoying making guns with the bricks and playing shooting games. The boys dominate the construction area with their gunplay. None of the three girls make any attempt to take part in these shooting games, although Jala and Ellie try to use the bricks. Ellie does not have a happy time when she tries to play in the construction area because Daniel tells her off for interfering with his gun. Jake is able to join the boys in the construction area by taking part in the gunplay. Ayan and Ellie both try to engage with the boys but are rebuffed. When the teacher comes into the area, the boys abandon their gunplay and start talking about shapes. The making of guns was not banned in this setting, but staff discouraged gunplay, and children usually pretended to be doing something else when a member of staff came near.

My fieldnotes over the two years of my research in Ash Vale show that boys took up most of the space and expected to dominate action in construction areas. Girls who played in the construction areas often became discouraged and chose to go to the book corner, writing area or roleplay area. Can this be described as a free choice? I think not. If we look closely at what is happening we can see that some boys are controlling play in the construction areas and making it difficult for girls to have an enjoyable time there. Jala, Ayan and Ellie wanted to play in the construction area but were put off by the boys' behaviour. Does it matter that some boys dominate play in construction areas? After all, you might say, some girls dominate play in roleplay areas. I believe it does matter, because it is limiting individual children's choices at a very early age. If we understand how and why children feel that they cannot engage in certain activities and must engage in others because they think they are only for boys or only for girls, we can develop strategies to support children in doing new things. It is important to talk to young children about their gendered behaviours and choices, and understand how children in early years settings learn play practices from each other.

Early years educators and parents tell me that they encourage boys and girls to choose activities freely, regardless of gender, but that most boys and girls naturally have different interests and are essentially different. It is this view that I challenge here. This book explores the reasons young children make gendered play choices and looks at how children position themselves within gender discourses and what they learn about the importance of gender in early years settings. It examines where and when boys and girls play with each other, and what happens when they do.

The term *gender dualism* refers to ideas which suggest that boys and girls are naturally different. Much early childhood educational research illustrates how influential ideas of gender dualism are. For example Ofsted's *Report on the Foundation Stage in 144 settings* (2007) found that girls were achieving better in all areas of the early years curriculum. Ofsted (Office for Standards in Education) is the official government body for inspecting schools in UK. The report suggests that boys are not achieving as well as girls because practitioners are not taking sufficient account of the ways in which boys learn. Boys, we are told, need more adult support than girls to develop their language and extend their play. The report says many boys choose not play with girls, and choose competitive raiding games involving physical gestures and running around whereas girls choose co-operative domestic play. The Report draws heavily on ideas of gender dualism. We are told that girls 'chatter to themselves and others' while boys 'need to be physically active'. Boys are positioned as naturally boisterous and physically active, in contrast to girls, who are positioned as naturally chatty, less active and more restrained.

The danger of generalisations based on gender dualism is that they ignore differences in individual children. As the 2007 Ofsted Report does, they often focus attention on the needs of boys, to the detriment of girls, by suggesting that special strategies are required to teach boys, whereas girls are doing fine. By encouraging practitioners to concentrate on boys as a group, the needs of girls – and some boys – are overlooked. All children need opportunities for active outdoor play and play that extends and develops their imagination and language, and some will need specific support. The Ofsted Report does not explore power relations and is therefore unable to account for children's gendered experiences.

Young boys and girls learn that certain masculine and feminine ways of behaving will earn them approval and status with other children and adults. Children learn to behave in different ways as boys and girls because doing so reflects the wider practices and values of the communities to which they belong. The challenge for us as educators is to intervene to help young children explore their feelings and understandings about gender, so that children can make choices beyond the stereotypes of gendered behaviours.

Development of gender identities

Children at Play explores how young children develop gender identities in the early years of schooling. The rich data from my two year school-based research study shows how children learned about gender from each other in social situations. Three and four year-olds in early years classes learned to play at different activities in their same-sex groups. These young children learned from each other that they needed to position themselves as correctly masculine or feminine in order to be accepted by other children, even though this limited their play choices.

I aim to explore how early childhood educators can work with young children in ways that promote equity and social justice. We need to look at young children's power relationships so we can understand the contexts in which gender identities are developed. My focus is on gender, but I also take account of ways in which gender relates to ethnicity, class and cultural differences. Young children are very aware of all these differences and struggle to make sense of them. Young children interact in many complex ways in their play relationships. They are continually exploring and learning about how to position themselves as a boy or a girl in various situations. We see how children use body postures, speech, knowledge about activities and spaces to negotiate power relationships and access to play scenarios.

Discussion

Read the extract from my fieldnotes on p.ix again.

As you read, think about how the children behave towards each other.

Do the boys and the girls behave differently?

Feminist poststructuralist theory

Researchers generally explain children's gendered behaviour in accordance with established suppositions and views. I challenge and even refute some of these assumptions so I need a new discourse with which to explore gendered behaviour. The terms I use appear first in italics and are explained in the Glossary of terms on page 135. I use *feminist poststructuralist* ideas in this book because they offer a way of moving beyond opposites of gender dualism.

MacNaughton (2000) gives a clear description of the limitations of biological and socialisation theories of how young children learn gender, and as I recommend you read her book I summarise only the main points here. Biological explanations for gender differences maintain that boys and girls, men and women are essentially different from each other, not just physically but also in the social roles they perform. Boys are seen as naturally more aggressive and girls as naturally quieter and more compliant. These biological explanations fail to take account of the range of individual behaviour and are often used to justify social inequalities. Socialisation theories argue that children develop gender identities from messages given by significant others and by observing and absorbing how people around them behave. This assumes that identity is fixed and coherent, and fails to answer the question of why it is that children accept some ideas and reject others.

Feminist poststructuralist theory offers us a way of understanding that the development of gender identity is an ongoing process, formed within social situations. Relationships between individuals and social institutions are seen to be inseparable, and interdependent, and power is seen as a central dynamic in relationships (Weedon, 1999). Drawing on poststructuralist theory, we can understand that children are competent participants within their social world. In constructing identities, children make use of meanings that are available to them. Some of these meanings are more powerful than others, because they are more available, more desirable or more pleasurable. As Davies (1998) and MacNaughton (2000) argue, children do not just soak up identity from social institutions and people around them. Young children reshape and develop individual identities as they engage with the diverse, and often contradictory, messages they receive from caregivers, at home, from the media, and in preschool settings. They learn very early from the re-actions of people around them what is acceptable or unacceptable in various situations. Children have to make their own meanings and make choices about what to do.

In feminist poststructuralist theory, the different ways of making meanings are called *discourses*, a term used throughout the book. The following play episode illustrates how children draw on discourses. Daniel (in his second term in Nursery) and Tia (in her first term) are in the play house in the garden. The teacher, Mrs Teal, is nearby. Daniel polices Tia's choice of a footballer's tabard, insisting that football is for boys.

> Daniel: (indicating Tia) 'She's taking off her coat.'
>
> Mrs Teal: 'That's ok because she's putting on a tabard.'
>
> Daniel: 'No, but that's for boys. Boys are footballers.'
>
> Mrs Teal: 'She can be a lady footballer. There are ladies' football teams as well as men's teams.'
>
> Daniel: 'No, it's men's football. Ladies don't play real football.'
>
> Tia quietly takes off the football tabard and starts a cheerleader dance with the pompoms instead.
>
> Daniel goes on to talk about football games he has seen on TV and names famous male footballers.

The children are trying to make sense of the different messages they are receiving. So what are the discourses Daniel and Tia are drawing on?

■ Daniel draws on a discourse of masculinity that says football is for boys. This is a powerful message in the Nursery, as older boys dominate football games and exclude the girls. It is also a powerful discourse in the world beyond Nursery, and Daniel draws on this when he argues with Mrs Teal, pointing out details of male footballers and men's football games he has watched on TV at home.

■ Tia is keen to have a go at positioning herself as a footballer, but to succeed she will have to be very persistent because of the powerful messages she receives that say football is for boys and men. As her teacher points out, girls and women do play football, but Tia immediately gives up her attempt to wear the footballer tabard whilst Daniel and his teacher are having their discussion. Instead she picks up the pompoms and starts a cheerleader dance. This dance is often performed by the older girls in Nursery and Tia has seen them earlier that day. The dance is modelled on the High School Musical sequences that were popular at the time of my research. Tia has seen High School Musical films in the cinema and on DVD at home. So we see that she draws on discourses of femininity that say dancing and cheerleading are for girls and she has taken on these messages from older girls in Nursery and from media images at home.

Observation exercise

Observe a free play episode in a construction area and a roleplay area in your early years setting.

Who dominates play? How do they achieve control?

Who is experiencing pleasure? Who is excluded?

What does this tell you about how boys and girls are learning about gender through their play activities?

Discourses

Drawing on the work of Foucault (1978, 1980), I use discourse to refer to social, institutional and emotional frameworks and practices through which humans make meanings of their experiences. A discourse refers to a way of speaking, writing, interacting or thinking that is made up of particular given truths that define what can and cannot be included, said or done (Paechter, 1998). Some discourses enable specific groups to exercise power in ways that benefit them, and others provide challenges to the *status quo*. Available discourses are often contradictory or conflicting.

My research adds to the body of feminist research that explores how young children position themselves within power and knowledge relations. Feminist educational researchers have drawn on Foucault's concepts of discourse, power and knowledge to theorise gendered power relations and to analyse young children's gender interactions (Davies, 1989; Walkerdine, 1990; Epstein, 1997; MacNaughton, 2000).

Walkerdine (1989) showed how young preschool boys were able to use a gender discourse of sexist objectification and harassment to enact a powerful position as males, in relation to a girl in their class, and to their female teacher. 'Miss Baxter, show off your bum. Show your knickers your bum off' (Walkerdine, 1989:65). Walkerdine reported that the teacher merely told the boys not to be silly and later described their behaviour as normal for their age. Although the boys were positioned as less powerful in relation to their teacher within the discourses of schooling and childhood, they were able to position themselves as powerful in relation to the teacher as a woman. Walkerdine's work emphasises how young children are positioned in different ways within different discourses and how some discourses can lead teachers to trivialise oppressive sexist language and behaviours.

Davies (1989) showed how young children learn to use knowledge about signifiers such as dress and activities to position themselves correctly as boys and girls. She showed how children negotiated power relations and negotiated contradictory gender discourses. She explored the importance of children's constructions of narratives and fantasy play in creating gendered identities and she argued that contradictions 'provide the creative cutting edge with which individual identities are formed' (Davies, 1989:29).

MacNaughton (2000, 2005) drew on poststructuralist Foucauldian theory to deconstruct discourses of early childhood education and analysed young children's gendered interactions in Australian preschools. She explored the range of masculine and feminine positions available to children in specific preschool settings.

A powerful discourse in early years education is that young children learn best through self-directed experimental free play, with minimal adult intervention. Free play encompasses voluntary, active, pleasurable, freely chosen, spontaneous play (Garvey, 1990). Piagetian discourses emphasise that children's free play is their work and it is thus seen as an important developmental stage in their learning. This has led to dominant developmental discourses in early childhood education that suggest practitioners should not interfere in children's free play, with the result that children's inequitable power relations have not been addressed (Walkerdine, 1989; MacNaughton, 2000).

Learning masculinities and femininities within power and knowledge relations

> Power is everywhere, not because it embraces everything, but because it comes from everywhere. (Foucault, 1978:93)

How do young children learn to construct masculinities and femininities within local power and knowledge relations? Although my focus is on gender identity it is important to consider the relational aspects of the development of children's identity. The concepts of race, ethnicity, class, sexuality, ability and gender are socially constructed and their meanings are reproduced and redefined within specific geographical and historical locations. I understand the development of social identities as an ongoing process of construction through intermeshing of different aspects of social relations, in specific historical contexts (Hall, 1992, 1996; Archer, 2003). Dimensions of gender, *ethnicity, race*, sexuality and class are relational, intertwined and combined, giving meaning to each other, and produced in specific lived situations. Power relations and inequity cannot be addressed by separating out different aspects of identity: it is important to consider them as relational (Gilroy, 1993; Mirza, 1992; Walkerdine *et al*, 2001; Robinson and Jones Diaz, 2006). 'It is in honouring our diversities of gender, 'race', class, ability, sexuality, age, geography and language that social justice, democracy and equity become possibilities'(MacNaughton, 2005:38). The dimension of power relations is crucial to understanding how racism, as well as sexism, operates between individuals and at an institutional level.

Discussion of terms

I understand 'race' to be a social construction that implies unequal power relations between different groups of people and use Gaine and George's working definition of 'race' as 'a group of people who may share some physical characteristic to which social importance is attached', and 'racism' to refer to 'belief that one 'race' is superior to others, coupled with power to put this belief into practice' (Gaine and George, 1999:5). I use 'ethnicity' or 'ethnic group' to refer to a group of people who share certain aspects of culture, such as religion, language and customs (Archer, 2003).

I draw upon Foucault's understandings of *power* and *knowledge* in my analysis of young children's gender constructs. Foucault (1977, 1978) conceives of power as both a productive and a repressive force, and argues that the study

---

of local practices can show how power operates at specific moments in relations between individuals through the discourses that circulate.

> It is in discourse that power and knowledge are joined together ... Discourse transmits and produces power; it reinforces it, but also undermines and exposes it, renders it fragile and makes it possible to thwart it. (Foucault, 1978:100/101)

Foucault emphasises that power is exercised in micro situations, in interactions between individuals, and argues that where there is power, there is also resistance (Foucault, 1978).

Following Foucault, I do not conceive power to be merely an exercise of force where one person or group makes other people do something. Power is omnipresent within networks of relationships, in struggles over how we give meanings to our lives, in how we are positioned and position ourselves within discourses. Institutionalised 'truths' are produced and reproduced in ways that govern and regulate us through the organisation of fields of knowledge. For example, discourses of education, psychology and medicine regulate, classify, categorise and organise people in relation to a set of 'truths' about what is normal or abnormal, healthy or unhealthy. These 'truths' are maintained and reproduced partly through individuals' self-surveillance and self-correction to established norms of behaviour.

> ...there is no need for arms, physical violence, material constraints. Just a gaze. An inspecting gaze, a gaze which each individual under its weight will end up interiorising to the point that he is his own overseer, each individual thus exercising this surveillance over, and against himself. (Foucault, 1977: 155)

Following Foucault, Bordo (2004) notes that power relations between men and women can be seen to be reproduced through self-normalisation to everyday practices of femininity and masculinity. For example diet and exercise regimes train the female body to be docile and obedient to certain cultural norms, giving individual women and girls feelings of being in control and powerful, whilst at the same time objectifying female bodies and positioning women as objects available for male pleasure (Bordo, 2004). This book explores how young children in Ash Vale engaged in practices of self-surveillance and self-correction.

Foucault emphasises that power relations are inseparable from other types of relationships (knowledge, sexual relationships, economic processes) and that 'power is exercised from innumerable points, in the interplay of nonegalitarian and mobile relations' (Foucault, 1976:94). Discourse can be an instrument and an effect of power, but also a point of resistance. Foucault sees resistance arising most productively at points where power relations are most rigid and intense. So, for example, Foucault shows how the sexed body is a target of disciplinary power, and how homosexuality has been a site for resisting techniques of disciplinary power. Foucault's analysis of 18th and 19th century sexualities, particularly with regard to homosexuality, gives insights into the complex interplay between the production of subjects who are positioned within disciplinary regimes, and who are simultaneously resisting or reworking these positions.

Foucault argues that some 19th century discourses such as the pedagogic report and medical examination apparently function to prohibit wayward or unproductive sexualities, but can be seen to function also as mechanisms with an impetus to both pleasure and power, evidenced in what Foucault graphically describes as 'perpetual spirals of power and pleasure' (Foucault, 1976: 45), for example, in relations between doctors and patients, parents and children, educators and students. Foucault demonstrates the complex power relationships involving, on the one hand, the pleasure that comes from exercising a power that watches, monitors and searches things out, as for example performed by a psychiatrist and, on the other hand, the pleasure that arises from evading, fooling, scandalising or resisting this kind of examination or interrogation.

> These attractions, these evasions, these circular incitements have traced around bodies and sexes, not boundaries to be crossed, but perpetual spirals of power and pleasure. (Foucault, 1976:45)

Throughout this book we see how young children in Ash Vale were involved in spirals of power and pleasure, in their relationships with each other, and with adults in the setting.

1

Researching with young children

To do feminist research is to put the social construction of gender at the center of one's inquiry ...Through the questions that feminism poses and the absences it locates, feminism argues the centrality of gender in the shaping of our consciousness, skills and institutions as well as in the distribution of power and privilege. (Lather, 1991:71)

This book is based on a longitudinal research project conducted with young children in early years classes in a London Primary school over two years. I sought to contribute to feminist understandings of how young children develop gender identities in the early years of schooling. This chapter describes the research setting and introduces the children involved. It explains my research methods and discusses ethical and methodological issues that arise from doing research with young children.

Research questions

My key research questions were:

- what discourses of femininity and masculinity do young children draw on in the early years of schooling?
- how do young children embody and perform masculinities and femininities in their activities and relationships in the early years of schooling?

I examined how the children experienced pleasure and power, how they used fantasy, stories and imaginative play to develop ideas about gender, and how their understanding of gender affected their play. I wanted to find out about the children's ideas about their own and other people's gender, and how schooling practices affected their behaviour as a boy or a girl. I was particularly interested in exploring how children who were new in school learned about practices of masculinity and femininity and how they resisted or conformed to gender norms.

Design of study

I had several reasons for choosing Ash Vale. Initial conversations with staff suggested that gender equity was an important issue, and I felt comfortable when I spent time in the school because children and adults were very welcoming. The school's population was comparatively stable and most of the children who attended the Nursery went on to the Reception class, so I could expect to follow groups of children over two years. The school was close to my home so I could visit frequently. I followed cohorts of children from Nursery into Reception to see how their ideas and behaviour developed as they moved from Nursery to Reception. I used qualitative research methods, based on participant observation of pupils in the Nursery and Reception classes.

Research context
The School

'Ash Vale' (pseudonym) is an inner city state primary school in London, drawing its pupils from the adjoining 1930s local authority housing estate. It had 250 boys and girls aged 3 to 11 on roll. Pupils came from the local, culturally diverse community. The largest group was of Black African heritage and there were a number of children from recently arrived refugee and asylum seeker families. Over half the pupils at the school spoke a language other than English as their first language. The socio-economic circumstances of many families were described in the school's Ofsted Report (2006) as 'not favourable' and over three quarters of pupils were eligible for free school meals (an indicator that the family has a low income). The Ofsted Report indicated that a large number of pupils joined and left each year, many pupils entered school with limited English, and the proportion of pupils with learning difficulties and disabilities, including those with statements of special educational needs, exceeded the national average.

Nursery and Reception classes

There were ten full-time places and 30 part-time places in the Nursery for children aged 3 and 4. Children who had a part-time Nursery place attended either in the mornings or the afternoons. The Reception class (for children aged 4 to 5) took 30 children in two intakes each academic year, up to half in September and the remainder in January. Full-time Nursery places were allocated chiefly on the basis of age, mostly to older children the term before they were due to enter Reception. Most, but not all, children who attended Nursery went on to attend the Reception class at Ash Vale.

The Nursery and Reception classes each had their own indoor classroom and outdoor play area. The Nursery had a garden area. During the lunch break Reception and Year 1 children shared two play spaces, and full-time Nursery children joined them for the first half hour. Children in Nursery and Reception classes had several periods of whole class teaching each day 'on the carpet', where all the children sat together on a carpet facing the teacher. For the rest of the day, children were taught in small groups, and encouraged to choose play based activities for themselves from a selection offered in the classrooms and outdoor areas. The Nursery class had one qualified teacher and one nursery nurse. The Reception class had one qualified teacher and one classroom assistant. Children were supervised at lunchtimes for an hour by mealtime supervisors. Special needs teachers, bilingual and other support assistants were allocated to the classes for some of the teaching time.

I gave pseudonyms to all children and staff to preserve anonymity.

Staff who appear in this book

Mrs Teal (Nursery teacher)

Mrs Jones (Nursery teacher)

Mrs Clarke (Nursery teacher)

Ms Foster (Reception teacher)

Ms Daly (Reception teacher)

Ms Kent (Classroom Assistant in Reception)

Mrs Chen (Bilingual Assistant)

Ms Lucas (Meals Supervisor)

Children who appear in this book

All names are pseudonyms.

Details of home languages and ethnicity are as given to me by staff based on information from parents.

Girls	Background
Sara	Farsi
Sammie	English
Zuhre	Turkish
Ayla	Turkish
Yomi	English/Yoruba
Lan	Vietnamese

Girls	Background
Chloe	English
Ayo	English/Ijaw
Oni	Yoruba
Shona	English
Nina	Spanish
Madia	Spanish
Madison	English
Melek	Turkish
Hong	Chinese
Nadia	Somali
Molly	Ugandan
Tagan	English
Tia	English/Yoruba
Jala	Krio
Eser	Turkish
Fifi	Yoruba
Zoe	English
Marsha	English (Ghanaian)
Lisa	English
Amena	English
Paige	Twi
Fatima	Turkish
Ayan	Somali
Leonie	English/Yoruba
Ellie	English
Alita	Spanish/Benin

Boys	Background
Ravi	Bengali
Reece	English
Jake	English
Harrison	English/Yoruba
Mani	Tamil
Femi	Yoruba
Omar	Turkish
Kumi	Yoruba
Jing	Cantonese
Tarak	Bengali

Boys	Background
Lewis	Twi/English
Ryan	English
Daniel	English/Yoruba
Tu	Vietnamese
Ben	English
Damien	English
Malik	Somali
Ervin	Albanian
Adil	Malayan
Ade	Yoruba
Jason	Twi/English
Liam	English
Jo	English
Charlie	English
Philip	English
Richard	English/Yoruba
Ho	Cantonese
Emilio	Spanish/Benin
Leon	English

Methodology and ethical considerations

My belief that gender is socially constructed determined my choice of methodology. I share MacNaughton's feminist aim of engaging with young children and early years educators to expand their ways of seeing and doing gender (MacNaughton, 2000, 2005). She emphasises that young children's development of gender identity takes place through interaction with others, and the constructs they can develop are limited to the alternatives that are available to them.

> In constructing identities, children access the particular meanings available to them and then: read them, interpret them, live them, embody them, express them, desire them, gain pleasure through them, understand them, take them up as their own. (MacNaughton, 2000:25)

Feminist researchers including Danby (1998), Davies (1989), Renold (2005) and Blaise (2005) have demonstrated children's competence as players in their social world, showing how they use play practices to establish social groups. My study adds to this work and follows a sociology of childhood framework that perceives children as capable of producing competent versions of their own lived experience (Mayall, 2002; Farrell, 2005). This is in contrast to

5

approaches of early childhood researchers who believe that young children are unable to give consent because they are not old enough to comprehend what they are being asked to do.

I support the growing tradition of participatory research with children, as opposed merely to observing them (Christensen and James, 2000; Connolly, 1998). In the 20th century, the concept of children's rights encouraged the development of research methods and research agendas that value children's abilities and social competences and understand children as active social players (Mayall, 2002). Feminist researchers including Davies (1982) and Thorne (1993) used ethnographic methods to study details of childhood cultures and power relations to show that children actively construct their own cultures.

I see children as active social players, and believed I had a responsibility to the children who took part in my research project, to work with them, listen to their ideas with respect, and explain my intentions as fully as possible (MacNaughton, 2005; Blaise, 2005). I aimed to promote children's rights during the research process, by ensuring they had safe spaces and privacy to share their ideas, choices over how and when to respond, and ownership over the data and ideas generated. Thus I saw the children as research players and decision makers in their own right.

Power, knowledge and representation

Different research methodologies provide different claims for the knowledge produced. I drew on ethnographic and discourse analytic methods, and these can employ different ideas about language. Traditional ethnography has presented research findings as empirical studies, gaining authority from the observational skills and rigorous processes of analysis of the researcher. The role of the researcher in ethnography is seen as to interpret and describe the meanings and functions of people's behaviour in specific communities and contexts. Language is understood as the medium for conveying and portraying what the researcher has discovered in fieldwork. In the first volume of a new journal *Ethnography*, the following description shows the central philosophy of ethnography.

> ...it is a family of methods involving direct and sustained social contact with agents, and of richly writing up encounter, respecting, recording, representing at least partly in its own terms, the irreducibility of human experience. Ethnography is the disciplined and deliberate witness-cum-recording of human events. (Willis and Trodman, 2000:7)

I used methods from ethnography to study children's actions and interactions. Whilst I aimed to use rigorous processes of data collection and
analysis, I do not claim that my findings can portray how things are, objec-
tively. Drawing on feminist poststructuralist theory, I hold that knowledge is
constructed through language and social practices. Accordingly, my role as a
researcher is to show how different kinds of knowledge are produced within
power relations in the social contexts I studied. Social meanings are produced
within social institutions and social practices. The meanings of social practices are sites of ongoing power struggles so it is not possible to fix meaning
once and for all (Weedon, 1987). As Weedon argues, we have access to a range
of discursive positions and these positions are often conflicting and inscribed
with different power relations.

I drew on feminist research methodology for my emphasis on deconstruction
of discourses and I used feminist poststructuralist methods of discourse
analysis (Baxter, 2003) to explore the multiple positions and complexities of
shifting power relationships in young children's experiences of gender in preschool. How I am positioned, and position myself, in discourses is directly
related to the knowledge I produce as a researcher. Reflexivity is a central
feature of my research process. Ribbens and Edwards (1998) claim that
feminist reflexivity involves explicitly taking into consideration the operation
of power within research processes. They argue that researchers who work
with children need to take into consideration how power operates through
hegemonic cultural perspectives during the research process. These operations of power are contained in the adult centred language we use, the adult
positions we take up during research in the field, and through the specific
individual relationships we make with children during research. I tried to
make my own positions, assumptions and emotional investments as clear as
possible to the children I worked with, and in the writing up of my findings.

As a feminist researcher working with young children, I faced the dilemma
shared by many feminist researchers who want to represent the voices of research participants in ways that are faithful to the research participants' language and experiences, while not positioning them as Other or reproducing
hierarchies of power and knowledge (Ribbens and Edwards, 1998). Researchers who use traditional approaches, for example in analysis of interviews, sometimes mask the relations of power that are inherent in the research
relationship, by claiming representational status for their own perspective.
This is a hegemonic aspect of Western scientific discourse, and is so entrenched that it appears natural. Research findings are presented as though
they are objective, when they are actually dependent upon how the researcher

is positioned. For example, Corsaro's research with young children aims to escape from an adult world and enter the child's world (Corsaro, 1981). He presents his findings as a realistic portrayal of children's culture, as if this observed culture existed, independent of his researcher's gaze, available to be reported. A poststructuralist approach understands language as constitutive and productive rather than simply reflective (Alldred, 1998). Researchers have power in the ways they select, interpret and produce meanings through language, and in the presentation of my findings I aim to show how I have selected and shaped my data.

Ethical issues in research with young children

I followed BERA and BSA ethical guidelines: 'All educational research should be conducted with an ethic of respect for: the Person, Knowledge, Democratic Values and The Quality of Educational Research' (BERA, 2004:5). I faced moral dilemmas when deciding when to intervene in children's conversations and actions. My priorities were to respect the children and to avoid doing anything that would be likely to harm or distress them. It is important that some children are not silenced. I wanted to enable children to speak for themselves, but not to provide spaces for some children to act in racist and sexist ways, without challenging such behaviour (MacNaughton, 2005). I would have thought it right to break children's confidentiality if what they told me made me think they were at risk of harm.

Data are a social construct of the research process (Ball, 1990). He makes the important point that researchers need to consider how their own role has influenced their research participants and the ways they have collected data, as this will affect analysis. Ribbens and Edwards (1998) and Narayan (1989) argue that feminists need to adopt high standards of reflexivity and openness about the choices we make at every stage of an empirical study, including how we hear interviewees and represent them in data analysis and writing up. This involves recognition that our own positions make a difference to the knowledge we produce, and that we have to make judgements about the best ways of communicating this knowledge to others. Narayan (1989) terms this a 'perspectival' view of knowledge. This seems to me to be a useful approach because it aims to make power relations and decisions transparent but avoids the paralysing conclusion that research should not take place at all, because of the problems of representation.

Moral dilemmas arise from the power relationships between the researcher, as an adult, and the research participants, as children. Many feminist researchers working with young children have reflected on this power im-

balance, and made various attempts to mitigate it or to give it due consideration. As Thorne asserts, she as a researcher is a spectator, even at times a
voyeur, despite her respect for the children, '... for my gaze remained, at its
core and in its ultimate knowing purpose, that of a more powerful adult'
(Thorne, 1993:27).

In using methods of participant observation with young children, researchers
have deliberately adopted a 'least adult role', so as to minimise the power differential and encourage children to open up, talk and behave as they would if
the researcher were not present (Davies, 1989; Thorne, 1993; Epstein, 1998).
'The least adult role' is when an adult behaves as if they were a child themselves. This method has produced a wealth of interesting data, and I used it
myself, but it is fraught with difficulties. A researcher must train herself not to
intervene in interactions, to be reactive rather than active, so as not to direct
what happens (Epstein, 1998). Children frequently appeal to a researcher as
an adult, to help sort out problems, discipline other children, and help with
work. As Epstein points out (1998), the researcher in primary school is positioned as one of a small number of adults responsible for the care and control
of large numbers of children. As an adult, the researcher does have a different
status within the school, and is able to draw upon personal knowledge and
authority.

Epstein (1998) points to another difficulty: although adopting 'least adult role'
is an attempt to reduce the power differential, it can it in some ways reinforce
it because it imposes this construction on the children when they might
prefer to position the researcher in a more familiar adult role, such as teacher,
carer or Mum. I adopted all these roles at different times in my research
settings, and I wondered how this affected the data I produced. I was also
aware that I could revert to being a powerful adult when I chose, and either
remove myself from a situation or intervene. Epstein (1998) gives a telling
example of this from her reading of Davies (1989). Davies describes herself as
taking part fully in the children's world in a game where she takes power as
'Queen of the World' when she is positioned by some boys as powerless-as-
female. Epstein points out that the boys might have been furious with her
because they were resisting her adult power.

The historical context is also an issue. I place my research within the growing
field of childhood studies that understand childhood as a social construction
(James and Prout, 1997; Mayall, 2002; Kehily, 2004). '...The immaturity of children is a biological fact of life but the ways in which it is understood and made
meaningful is a fact of culture' (James and Prout, 1997:7). I draw on social on

constructions of childhood that perceive childhoods as periods of lived experience, rather than just preparations for adulthood, and constructions of
children that emphasise that they are persons in their own right, competent
social players with their own distinctive cultures (Mayall, 2002; George, 2007).

There are many discourses of childhood, serving a variety of purposes (Mayall,
2002). The notion of a stage of life termed 'childhood' has had different meanings ascribed to it at different times (James and Prout, 1997). These include
discourses of so-called natural childhood where children were seen variously
as essentially either innocent or evil, or as a *tabula rasa* (blank slate) in need
of nurture, training, discipline or control, so they could become civilised
adults.

In the 18th and 19th century conflicting and contradictory discourses of childhood developed that reflected and reproduced the values and practices of the
European middle classes. Girlhood, in particular, was often represented by
associations with nature and vulnerability, in line with Romantic discourses
(Walkerdine, 2004). Childhood has been seen as a stage of life when we require
care and protection in our innocence, and the discourse of the innocent child
continues to be influential in educational and social policies and institutional
practices (Renold, 2005; Robinson and Jones Diaz, 2006).

The post-1945 British primary school projected a safe space, a greenhouse
where children could develop in a protected environment. This was also the
rationale behind the establishment of British nurseries – with outdoor open
play spaces in urban areas – where young children could develop naturally as,
in Froebel's metaphor, 'buds unfurling in a garden' (Moss and Penn, 1996). As
Connolly (2003) argues, young children's play is not always innocent and
school playgrounds can be unsafe spaces for children, who may be subjected
to bullying and sexist, homophobic and racist abuse. But discourses of innocent childhood often influence early years practitioners so they are reluctant
to intervene in children's play in the playground.

The empirical study of children in the West since the 19th century has been
regarded as the domain of psychology. Research in developmental psychology has focused on the individual child as an object of study, and attempts to
document and understand how children develop through a sequence of
stages culminating the use of abstract reasoning. This developmental discourse sees childhood as preparation for adulthood, with children progressing through age-related stages, as 'becomings' rather than people in their
own right (Walkerdine, 2004). These cultural constructions of childhood influence the way research with young children has been conducted.

Developmental discourses exacerbate children's objectification within research, and they can be used to discount what children say and do. Discussion of methodological issues in research with young children often suggests that children are unreliable research subjects because they confuse fact and fiction, lack logical reasoning skills, and tell adults what they think the adult wants to hear. For example, Grant (2002) argues that data from interviews with young children can be unreliable because they will say anything rather than nothing, and she cites Simons (1982) and Lewis (1992) in support. From a poststructuralist viewpoint, children are positioned within a discourse of incompleteness, in an adult-dominated culture. They have to make themselves meaningful in adult-centred terms.

I wanted to demonstrate that complexity, ambiguity and contradiction are inherent features of language rather than just the result of children's immaturity. I was aware that children might not find informal interviews with a researcher an empowering experience, in a context where they are expected to make sense to an adult, and where language is productive of adult power (Alldred, 1998). I found that children did sometimes try to say things to please me, but they also changed the subject or opted out if they became bored or uncomfortable (Aubrey *et al*, 2000). I tried to pick up on their cues to avoid causing distress, although I did, unwittingly, sometimes upset children. On one occasion, Zuhre cried when I said she must wait for a turn to work with me. My insistence that children opt in to work with me was designed to prevent their feeling pressurised to do so, but the practical problem turned out to be that too many at once wanted to engage with me in an activity.

Details of research methods
I used ethnographic methods to find out about the children's play practices through participant observation, data collection and analysis based on two years of fieldnotes. I used methods of participant observation where I took part in activities based on stories, writing, drawing, construction and roleplay with individual children and small groups. I had ongoing discussions with children and adults in the settings, and conducted semi-structured interviews with children. I spent one day a week in school throughout the period, and made numerous additional visits on different days, varying the times so that I built up a picture of daily routines in Nursery and Reception classes.

I observed and documented how girls and boys used the space and resources, and how practices emerged from the structures. I observed and mapped who used different spaces in classrooms and playgrounds, who moved, where, and when. I documented how children moved, any constraints on their

physical movement, their choice of activities, and who was included or excluded from activities. I collected data about changing friendship patterns,
ways of speaking and bodily gestures. I observed how children who were new
to Nursery watched older children and copied aspects of their play, and documented their play patterns as they became established in Nursery. These
methods produced rich data on the children's behaviour and interactions,
and enabled me to focus on ways in which children are active agents in their
own learning (Mayall, 2002).

Taking detailed fieldnotes of children's play and conversations and making
sketches of the children's movements proved to be the most effective ways of
collecting data. I spent about half my time in each session joining in with children's activities, and the rest observing, sitting in different areas of the classroom or playground and making detailed sketches and notes of who played
in the area, what was said, who moved where, and how play episodes began
and ended. Carlspecken's (1996) method of priority observation helped me
ensure I collected data on all the children in the group. I followed each child
in turn for ten minute observations, noting what they said and did, their
movements, interactions, intonation and bodily gestures. I interrupted these
individual observations if a significant event such as a change in routine or
conflict caught my attention. I invited children to take part in some semi-
structured activities with me and I read stories with them, as a stimulus for
discussing their ideas and experiences of gender.

I brought into class a selection of capes for imaginative play and encouraged
the children to develop stories and imaginative play themes wearing them. I
used pictures of popular toys to stimulate discussion about favourite toys. I
invited Reception children to tell me about what they liked to play in the playground and talk about their experiences of lunchtime play. We recorded their
comments in their drawings, in my fieldnotes and sometimes on audiotape.
Children moved around a lot and the noise levels often obscured speech on
the taperecorder so taperecording gave me little data, although some of the
children enjoyed hearing their voices on the tape, and enjoyed interviewing
me and their classmates.

I also observed the children during periods of formal instruction, in teacher
directed Literacy and Numeracy lessons on the carpet, in PE lessons in the
main Hall, and in whole school assemblies. I discussed my research with early
years staff and asked them to comment on my data. I sent letters to parents
each term, outlining my research and inviting them to talk with me about it.

My position as adult researcher

Being an adult had implications for my role as researcher. I am physically much larger than the children, and I sometimes had the feeling I was taking up too much space in the Nursery, particularly when in a small space like the roleplay area. Children might experience my presence as intrusive, controlling, dominating, comforting, reassuring or confusing in different situations. I needed to be aware of this, and also aware that my physical presence in school spaces altered situations. Even when I was sitting quietly at the edge of the carpet, I was writing in my notebook, and children and staff would sometimes address comments to me that showed they were conscious of my watching them. I could not take part in some of the children's activities, even had they wanted me to, because I am not fit enough and am too big to use items like bikes, climbing frames and skipping ropes.

I could claim adult privileges as to how and when I joined the children. Nespor (1997) describes how he refused to reinforce children's gendered meaning of lunch tables, by declining the boys' request to sit on their table and sitting instead with the girls. He remarks that this 'probably just announced that I was claiming the adult's privilege of refusing to play the game' (Nespor, 1997: 135). When I was in the playground, children often came up and chatted to me and asked me to sit down with them. They were often keen to tell me about their games and liked writing and drawing in my notebook. Usually I complied, but at times I showed them my notes and drawings and told them I was busy writing my own notes. I kept some control of my activities, and, unlike them, I had the option of going indoors when I liked.

Researchers working with young children report that they have felt like a child themselves, and have drawn on their own memories of childhood to inform their work (Thorne, 1993; Epstein, 1998). This can be a strength, but everybody has a different experience of being a child, and we must not overestimate how much we can understand children's points of view just because we were once a child (Epstein, 1998). And our memories of our childhoods are not entirely reliable. As I recall, I was quite an obedient child, yet here I found myself wanting to encourage certain subversive behaviour in the children, particularly related to carpet time. I resisted these impulses, but I was careful to make it clear to the teachers and children that I was not in a position of authority in the school.

Some teachers tried to put me in a teacher role. But although I tried to be helpful with routine classroom tasks, I did not take on a disciplinary role. Staff were usually polite and sometimes even deferential, which surprised me. I conclude that they viewed my presence as non-threatening to them and beneficial to the children. That was certainly my intention. I always discussed my work with teachers and support staff and asked them to tell me if anything I did was unhelpful. If children asked me to intervene in disputes I usually referred them to a member of staff, saying I was not a teacher or lunchtime supervisor. Most children and staff accepted this and did not ask me to deal with discipline issues. I think the staff found me acceptable, partly because I was an older woman and a retired teacher.

As an experienced teacher, I found the role of researcher challenging. I had to learn to intervene far less and to relinquish control of activities. When engaged in stories and roleplay with the children, I was sometimes tempted to try and assert my authority as an adult, if not as a teacher. In the following fieldnote, I describe Marsha's behaviour when she tries to direct an activity as 'bossy'. I was drawing on a gendered discourse myself, as I would not have used this word to describe a boy.

Diary entry

As it was raining, the children couldn't go outside today, and there was a cover teacher as well, so I was more 'in demand' than usual. Children kept crowding round my table wanting a turn, and interrupting, and I had difficulty keeping focused myself. Marsha started getting very bossy at one point and telling children who would be next to have a turn with me and where they should sit. I said to her 'Marsha, wait a minute, are you in charge here?' She said no, and backed off, but I felt a mixture of alarm at being so bossy myself, and triumph in asserting control again. I do find it hard to get a balance, I don't want to be in teacher mode, but I do want to have some authority, so I can get them to focus on my research agenda, and so they get a fair turn if they want one. Playing back my tapes, it strikes me that I do sound calm, interested and encouraging. Which is a relief, because I quite often feel rather overwhelmed and harassed by the sheer number of demands for my attention.

I found myself trying to claw back some semblance of order in situations that felt too chaotic. I worried that staff would think we were making too much noise. I sometimes felt annoyed when some children tried to dominate proceedings, and I often felt overwhelmed by the demands on my attention and concentration. Above all, however, I felt enormous respect and admiration for the children I worked with, and I was moved by their trust in me and their willingness to share their experiences and thoughts. Some were keen to make sure I was happy with what I was learning from them, and tried hard to explain what they were doing in ways they thought I would understand. In the

14

following fieldnote I recorded how Ravi made me welcome at the start of his first term in Reception. I was feeling rather nervous myself, and it may be that Ravi saw this.

> Ravi: 'Miss! Barbara! I am in Reception now. Do you remember I was in Nursery I do stickers with you.'
>
> (Ravi shows me his alphabet book and demonstrates what he can read now.)
>
> Ravi (to BM): 'Are you happy now?'
>
> ... Ravi brings the junk model boat he has made and gives it to me.
>
> Ravi: 'This for you.'

The research process must avoid exploiting those who take part (Stanley and Wise, 1993). Accordingly, I needed to consider how to give both adults and children choices about whether and when they participated. Moral dilemmas occurred at every point. I promised to preserve the anonymity of all participants, but this proved incompatible with the important commitment to share my research findings. Despite the changed names, individual children and staff were recognisable to those who knew them, so I had to decide when to share my findings, and with whom. For example, I decided not to share some analysis of children's play episodes with staff, because I thought they might be annoyed with the children and this would be a betrayal of the children's trust in me.

Gaining the informed consent of young children during the research process is problematic. The children I worked with were often eager to participate, but it was difficult to explain to them what my work as a researcher entailed. Epstein (1998) describes how she tried to give her young research participants some information and control over their involvement. She showed them her notebook, invited them to ask her about what she wrote, and promised she would tear out an entry if they did not like what she had written. She promised not to show the notebook to the teachers, and tried to answer their questions honestly. Epstein also promised the head teacher that she would show him the finished research before publication, and as he would be able to recognise the children even with their names changed she could not really offer the children confidentiality. Even though they could make some decisions about when, and what, to tell her, Epstein argues that it was impossible for the young children to give informed consent to taking part in her research as they had no experience by which they could understand her role as a researcher. This is indeed a problem, and the concept of informed consent is problematic in ethnography, as the presence of the researcher, as an outsider who observes, changes the dynamics of the group. A judgement does have to be made as to whether the research is important enough to justify researching with young children whose capacity for informed consent is limited.

Epstein's experiences emphasised for me how difficult it is to empower young children in the research process, and also how children are not ultimately in control of how the researcher uses what they say in the later analysis and comment. So I was wary of giving promises to adults in the setting, as my first loyalties were to the children. I promised the teaching staff that I would discuss my research at all stages and give them feedback, but did not say I would show them everything I did. At the start of each stage of my fieldwork, I explained to the children that I am a researcher, not a teacher, and that they could choose whether they wanted to take part in my research. I said I was writing a book and was interested in what they like to do and play in pre-school and school. I did not emphasise my interest in gender as I did not want generalising responses based on gender dichotomy (Francis, 1998). By spending a lot of time with the children, I could listen and wait for them to show me about 'doing' boy and girl. Getting their gender behaviour right was important to them, and they often talked spontaneously about their understandings of gender dualism.

Despite their willingness to take part in activities with me and talk to me, I was aware that however much I tried not to pressurise the children, some felt obliged to please me. Some even tried to give me the answers they thought I wanted. At the very least, they had to put up with having me around in their class and playground. In the following fieldnote, Ayo tells me she does not want me to be with her class on this day. I interpret her remark to mean that she feels she has to be on her best behaviour if I am there. My reply illustrates the limitations of the children's choice to participate in my research. Ayo need not talk to me, but she cannot prevent me joining her in class.

> Ayo to BM: 'Barbara, I want you to go to the Nursery today. I'm not in a very good mood.'

> BM: 'Well, I'm with your Reception class today Ayo, but you don't have to talk to me if you don't want to. That's fine.' (Later she comes and asks to do a picture).

When I was reading stories and doing roleplay activities, I often chose the focus and steered discussions towards my own agenda when the children were determined to set their own. All human interactions involve power relationships, and in my data analysis, I took account of the context in which children made comments, and the dynamics of the relationships, including my own interventions. Connolly (1998) notes how 6 year-old boys behaved in group discussions with him: how they emphasised their physical competence for the benefit of this adult man as well as their own, and took pleasure in demonstrating adult knowledge. They discussed taboo topics involving violence, sex and swearing, thus countering the dominant discourses of childhood within the school and challenging Connolly's authority as an adult. He sees this as expressive of a power struggle between himself and the boys.

I was often aware of children wanting to demonstrate adult knowledge to me, and I think this was partly so they could gain status amongst other children, but partly to tell me they, not I, were the experts on their own lives. I think some of the girls related their knowledge about adult feminine behaviour to me because I am a woman. Once I happened to be wearing nail polish, and this generated lengthy discussions about makeup and appearance. Many girls initiated conversations with me about what I was wearing, their own clothes and the differences in our names, skin colour and family relationships. Zuhre was pleased that my name sounded like her grandma's Turkish name. Amena told me several times that she knew a Barbara at her church who sang with her, but that she was black, like Amena, not white like me. Ayo looked at my face when I was feeling stressed and hot and remarked 'You used to be white but now you are red!' Many children were very welcoming and took trouble to show me things and explain about their life in school and sometimes about their home life.

I wanted to explore how children drew upon experiences from family and home in the Nursery and Reception settings as they struggled to make sense of the new communities of practice in Nursery and Reception. This was difficult because I was not observing the children in their homes or researching communities of practice outside the school settings. I was interested in how the different communities to which they belong presented the children with similarities or contradictions, but I could not collect data about it unless they shared their thoughts with me. I asked children questions and encouraged them to draw pictures, take part in roleplay and talk when it seemed appropriate to do so, but I did not want to be intrusive or cause distress. I felt honoured when children chose to share aspects of their home experience, as when Omar told me about how he enjoyed visiting his grandparents and riding on his uncle's farm tractor in Turkey, and that he was proud of his family's Turkish name.

Stories provided a useful starting point for discussion, but many of the children did not speak English fluently. The fundamental problem was due to the institutional ideology and practices of the school. Children were not encouraged to speak or write in their home languages or discuss their home experiences. They learned that English is the only acceptable language in the classroom. The lack of status given to the children's home languages contrasted with the status given to French, which was taught to all the Nursery and Reception children. Many children were anxious to demonstrate their knowledge of the few French words they had learned in school. The school's equal opportunities stance aimed to encourage respect for cultural diversity but in practice it privileged white Anglo Saxon heritage in curriculum delivery. This created an institutional silence about ethnic, religious and cultural differences, and marginalised the children's home cultures (Pearce, 2005). I found this difficult, as it is contrary to my understanding of education and equity.

Children's consent should be sought at each stage of the research process (Farrell, 2005). As an adult, I was in a position of power: I had ultimate control over how I used the data the children supplied in interviews and activities. As a participant observer, I saw and heard things other adults were not privy to, and sometimes entered children's worlds by their invitation, but only partially, and not as a child. So I can only glimpse aspects of how they see themselves and their worlds (Paley, 1981). My privileged position as a visitor to the children's social world presented ethical dilemmas. I sometimes saw things I thought the children would not have wanted me to see and did not know I had seen. I could not discuss this properly with them, so I omitted some sections of data from my analysis. Of course they might have disliked things I wrote too, had they seen them, so this was not a satisfactory solution. I did discuss children's contributions to my research with them, but I retained control over the end product.

I also found myself getting into power struggles with children over the ownership of their data. I was committed to involving them in decisions about their data. By 'their data' I acknowledge, at a rational level, their ownership of work produced during the research process. However, I sometimes found myself reacting at an emotional level in the classroom, even begging individual children to let me have their drawings for my book.

Diary entry
I feel like I want to keep control of what they are drawing now, get them to draw people not patterns. There is a power struggle too over whether they will give

me the drawings or take them home. I try to let them have a proper unforced choice, but sometimes catch myself using manipulative tactics.

BM to Zuhre: 'Please can I have that picture for my book?

Zuhre: 'No, I want to take it home.'

BM: 'Oh, but I will be sad if I can't have a picture from you, Zuhre.'

Zuhre (smiles): 'OK you have this one' (gives me one of her pictures).

(She has already got several to take home, is what I was thinking. On reflection, I can't believe I said that. So much for giving them control over their input! I feel guilty and try to make amends at once.)

BM: 'That is kind of you Zuhre, but of course you take it home if you want to.' (I try to give it back to her, but she smiles and shakes her head. Oh dear!)

(This reminds me of the games my goddaughter and I play when I try to persuade her to let me have a turn with her rubber ring in the swimming pool or wear her jewellery. She sometimes refuses me and it is one way she has of exerting power in our relationship, so I encourage her to make the choice, but at the same time I feel myself getting a bit upset if she persists in refusing to share with me).

Even when I tried to give children ownership of their data, I could not always be certain that I had not put pressure on them to give me what I wanted.

Lan wants to take her picture home, but I persuade her to let me borrow it to take a copy for my book. Is this ok? Not sure, because perhaps I put too much pressure on her to say yes to me. Feel a bit bad. But it's such a great picture. Will check with her when I give the original back that it is ok by her if I put it in my book.

'My book' emphasises that the finished product will be mine. However careful we are, research with young children involves ethical problems over differences in power and experience between adult researcher and children (Francis, 1998).

Conclusion

The aim of my research in Ash Vale was to contribute to educational practice that promotes equity and social justice. It is important to listen to the voices of children, in the context of widening their access to a range of gender positions. I wanted my research findings to acknowledge the power relationships arising from my role as researcher (Weedon, 1987). Whilst wanting to contribute to representational politics, I also wanted to avoid reinforcing the notion of the psychological child, the subject of developmental discourse, by emphasising that children take up different subject positions within different discourses (Alldred, 1998). I aimed to address issues of how children's subjectivity is constructed through language and through discursive practices (Weedon, 1987) by exploring the range of discursive gender positions available to young children, as they struggled to make sense of what it means to be a girl or boy in the early years of schooling. The following chapters discuss my findings.

2

The development of gender identities

A person's masculinity or femininity is not innate, is not natural, but instead is something that is learned, constantly reworked and reconfigured, and enacted to the self and others. (Paechter, 2007:14)

'Doing' gender in contemporary Western society involves creating differences between boys and girls from the moment they are named a boy or girl. These differences are not essential or biological, but once the differences have been constructed, they are used to justify, reinforce and reproduce discourses of gender difference. Young children learn about *masculinities and femininities* within local power and knowledge relations. When they start school, young children need to establish themselves as legitimate participants in communities of femininity and masculinity by interpreting and generating meanings from the messages available to them, drawing on their experiences from home and those they encounter in the Nursery and Reception. Adults in school are often engaged in training young children to become successful pupils. They exist as powerful agents, giving leadership and affirmation to the children, rewarding them with praise or imposing sanctions for certain behaviour. Children often hear contradictory messages from different adults and children at school and at home, so they have to figure out and negotiate what behaviour is acceptable in certain contexts.

This chapter introduces key ideas used in this book to help understand how young children learn about gender and to develop ways of working with young children to support them in making play choices beyond gender stereotypes. In the introduction I argued that the idea that boys and girls are naturally different often stops us from understanding what is happening in early years classrooms, because we expect boys and girls to play in separate groups at different activities. When girls push dolls in buggies we smile and say 'that's what girls enjoy'. If boys are boisterous and take up space with fighting games, we frown and say 'boys will be boys' and think we cannot do much to change what is happening. In this book I challenge these assumptions about young children by examining what happens when children play, and I argue that we can help them make alternative choices. I show how children dominated or avoided particular spaces in classrooms and playgrounds, and how they used spaces and activities as important markers of femininity and masculinity in their play.

A central tenet of early childhood education is that young children learn best through self-directed experimental free play, with minimal adult intervention. The dominant developmental discourses in early childhood education consequently suggest that practitioners should not interfere in children's free play. The result is that children's inequitable power relations have not been addressed (Walkerdine, 1989; MacNaughton, 2000). Children's play reproduces power relations based on dominant gender discourses. Children need access to new discourses through which they can construct alternative femininities and masculinities. They are positioned within discourses as powerful or powerless, depending on the social relations of power operating in specific play situations. When children join early years classes they learn to position themselves as a boy or a girl by observing what established children do and joining in with play. Schooling practices often reinforce and encourage gender dualism.

Communities of practice

My findings show that children in early years classes learn rules for gendered behaviour from each other. I use Paechter's theoretical work (2007) on communities of practice to explore how young girls and boys become members of local communities of practice of masculinities and femininities.

A community of practice can be defined as a group engaging in a shared practice.

The term 'community of practice' was introduced by Lave and Wenger (1991) to describe the learning of apprentices. They emphasise that learning takes place in social contexts through *legitimate peripheral participation*, by which they mean that new members are permitted to take part in minor aspects of a central activity. They noted how apprentices in the butchers' and tailors' trades developed knowledge about practices, including social practices, and developed their own expertise, through observing more experienced members and through gradually being permitted to take a more central part in the activities of the group. New apprentices began their apprenticeship through legitimate peripheral participation by making minor contributions to the practices of the group. For example, apprentice tailors were allowed to do some of the sewing of the garments, but not the cutting out. If they successfully learned the relevant skills and knowledge, they gradually progressed to become full participants. As new members joined, the community itself was constantly reconstructed.

Paechter (2007) applies these ideas to masculinities and femininities. She argues that children learn what it is to be masculine or feminine through legitimate peripheral participation in communities of femininity and masculinity of older children and adults. At the same time, children take part in communities of practice of girls and boys of a similar age to themselves, as full participants. Boys can been seen as apprentice men, and girls as apprentice women, learning through observation and peripheral participation what it means to be a man or a woman in the local communities of practice in which they live. The naming of a baby as a boy or girl at birth places the child within a particular community of practice, and this performative naming results in differential treatment and expectations (Butler, 1993; Paechter, 2007). Children are seen from birth as legitimate peripheral participants in local communities of practice of femininities and masculinities. Certain behaviour is encouraged, ignored, praised or emphasised, depending on whether the child is a boy or a girl.

Newcomers to Ash Vale became legitimate peripheral members and then full members of communities of practice of boys and girls in Nursery and Reception classes. My analysis of the use of the play spaces supports research that shows that young boys and girls usually play in same sex groups, at different activities (Lloyd and Duveen, 1992; Browne, 2004; Ofsted, 2007). When new children came into Nursery they usually spent much of their time observing older children, and gradually joined in aspects of play. Usually they arrived in cohorts, at the beginning of Autumn and Spring terms, when older children moved into Reception.

There were ten full-time places in the Nursery and the full-timers were mostly the older children, who had a dominant presence. They were usually more familiar with Nursery routines, more skilled at activities and use of equipment, had more developed language skills, spoke English more confidently, and knew the formal and informal social rules. They had usually made friends in Nursery and were confident in the Nursery setting. They had learned how to show that they knew what behaviour was correct for boys and for girls, and were eager to teach new arrivals the rules. When children moved into Reception, a similar process took place: established Reception children taught new children about gendered play behaviour. Newcomers to Nursery and Reception observed the play practices of more established pupils, learning to use key objects of knowledge and to reproduce gendered behaviours.

Legitimate peripheral participation in Nursery activities

To become a member of a girls' or boys' Nursery community of practice in Ash Vale, the first important thing to know was whether you were a girl or a boy. Children learned that gender is dimorphic and fixed. Children showed that they knew they were a boy or a girl by playing with other children of the same sex. This might appear obvious – researchers can overlook it as a motivation to play in same-sex groups. Children who were new to Nursery often watched older children, sometimes for long periods of time, and then copied aspects of what they observed. Knowing whether you are a boy or a girl was a prerequisite for taking part in activities as peripheral members of one or other community of practice. Older children in the Nursery usually played in same-sex groups; new children observed this and tried to join the same-sex groups. In this way they became legitimate peripheral participants in the Nursery communities of practice. Below, Malik and Damien watch older boys playing with cars and later play with the cars themselves. Zoe watches an older girl, Tagan, at the water tray and copies her. Malik, Damien and Zoe are in their first term in Nursery.

> 9.25 Malik comes and stands at edge of construction carpet, watches Daniel, Ryan and Jake who are having a boisterous racing game with the cars. Malik watches for two minutes, then goes away.
>
> ...
>
> 10.02 Malik returns, looks at the boys playing cars, goes away.
>
> 10.03 Damien comes over, stands at edge of carpet watching the three boys who are racing the cars across the carpet, goes away.
>
> ...
>
> 10.45 Damien playing with cars on his own on the construction mat. Making revving sounds. Malik joins. Parallel play.
>
> ...

> Zoe is watching Tagan fill up bottles at the water tray. She takes a bottle and is copying Tagan. Tagan does not say anything to her, but allows her to play alongside.

Damien tries to join in games with older boys on the bikes.

> Nursery garden
>
> Damien running round following Ryan who is riding a bike.
>
> Damien (shouting):'I want a bike.'
>
> Damien gets hold of a bike for minute, but cannot manage to get on.
>
> ... Damien chasing Ryan on bike. Ryan ignores him.

One week later

> Garden
>
> Damien and Ben on trikes
>
> Damien to Ben (looking at him, trying to get his attention): 'Ready steady go!'
>
> Ben (no reaction).
>
> Damien: 'Come and get me!'
>
> Ben: 'I can get you. I'm a big boy.'
>
> (they go round and round in a circle).
>
> Ben (laughing): 'Ra, ra!'

Ben, as an established older boy, makes it clear that he will only play with Damien on his own terms, as the boss. The older children often ignored new children, or allowed them to copy them as long as they did not interfere with their games.

Separate activities for boys and girls in Nursery and Reception

Knowing they were a girl or boy was not enough in itself to become a member of a community of practice in Ash Vale. Children had to demonstrate that they were able to take part in the shared repertoire of practices (Paechter, 2007). A key object of knowledge was knowing about the things which were for boys and the things which were for girls. One way of demonstrating this knowledge was to do separate boy or girl activities. Another was to police the behaviour of other children. These two aspects were often linked, as children displayed knowledge of a particular practice and, at the same time, excluded children of the opposite sex from the activity. This was demonstrated most simply when boys opted to sit with other boys and avoided sitting next to girls, and vice versa. Some children went to great lengths to sit with their same-sex friends and avoided sitting next to somebody of the opposite sex on the carpet.

Areas of the classroom and activities were gender marked by the children, and specific objects and practices were used to delineate femininity and masculinity within the girls' and the boys' communities of practice. In art and collage activities, knowledge about fashion, play to do with families and home, Disney princess stories, Barbies, the colour pink, and dance were all markers of femininity, seen as things for girls. Construction, battle play, football games and knowledge of sport were markers of masculinity, seen as things for boys. I analysed the children's use of spaces in Nursery in detail. Plans A and B below show the gendered use of spaces in the Nursery classroom and outdoor play area during the first term of my research.

Some boys dominated and controlled access to construction areas. Some older girls dominated and controlled access to roleplay areas. The computers and the water trays and sandpit were used by both boys and girls. Boys dominated the area around the basketball net. The climbing frames were disputed territory.

Shared repertoire

According to Wenger (1998), to be a full participant in a community of practice, core meanings must be shared, there must be involvement in a shared repertoire of performances, a contribution to an ongoing practice, and accepted markers of membership. Wenger understands a community of practice as locally based. He argues that identities are developed and negotiated through the practices with which we engage and that mutual engagement, joint enterprise and a shared repertoire become central to our identity as we become participants in communities of practice. Paechter suggests that the most important aspect of this for communities of femininities and masculinities is the shared repertoire aspect of identity. She argues that in order to be accepted as fully masculine or fully feminine within a particular social group, it is important to perform and display specific characteristics and behaviours.

> Identity can in this way be seen as being related to competent and convincing performance of a particular role; it is defined not just internally by the individual but externally by the group's inclusive or exclusive attitude to that individual. (Paechter, 2003:74)

There were power struggles in Ash Vale as some oldtimers struggled to dominate activities and some children opted out or were excluded from participation. Local communities of practice are always in flux, and there is nothing

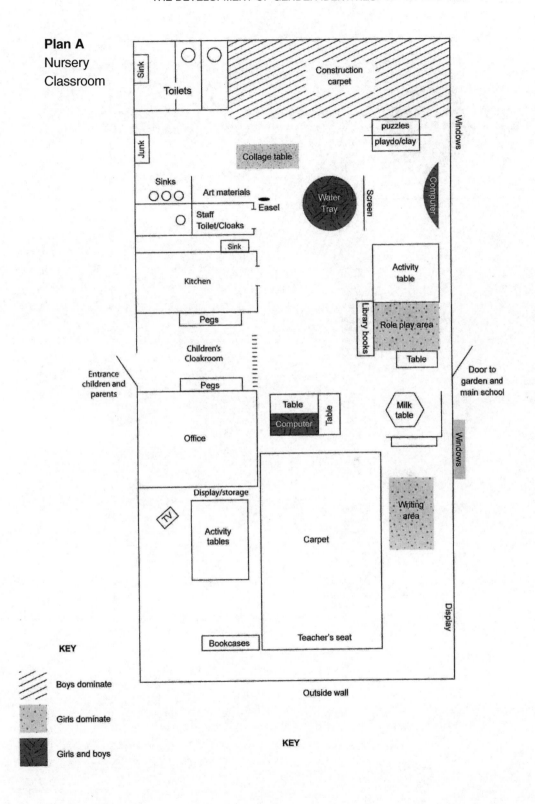

Plan A
Nursery
Classroom

KEY

Boys dominate

Girls dominate

Girls and boys

KEY

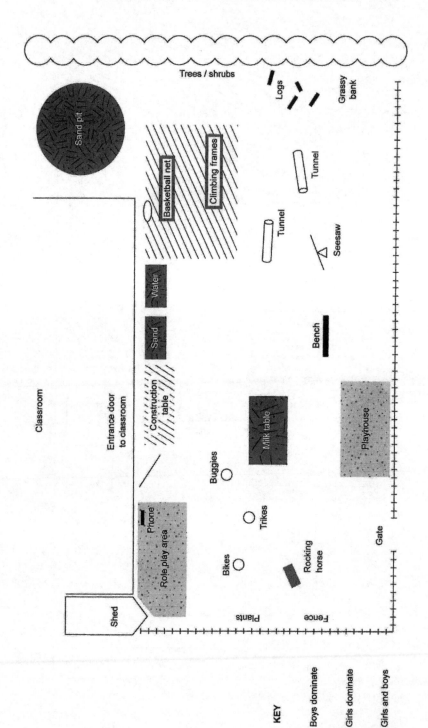

Plan B
Nursery Garden

inevitable about the process of becoming a member. I identified three stages to becoming a full member of a boys' or girls' community of practice. Firstly, in order to participate as a legitimate peripheral member, children needed to categorise themselves, and others, as either a boy or a girl. Secondly, they needed to participate in a shared repertoire of masculine or feminine activities. Thirdly, in order to influence the local practices of masculinity or femininity, they had to embody them and demonstrate that they knew and could use the appropriate gendered objects of knowledge. Using and embodying objects of knowledge is closely linked to gendered use of spaces. The children declared specific areas within the classroom and playground for boys or for girls and policed the access to them. Boys learned that knowledge about football was an important way to be accepted as a boy, and girls learned that taking part in skipping was important for girls.

Wenger sees individual identity as being developed through our participation in various communities of practice.

> Our various forms of participation delineate pieces of a puzzle we put together rather than sharp boundaries between disconnected parts of ourselves. An identity is thus more than a single trajectory; instead it should be viewed as a nexus of multimembership. (Wenger, 1998:158-159)

Paechter (2007) applies this to the way that individuals become members of different overlapping communities of practice of femininities or masculinities, and points out that these identities are just one aspect of our sense of self. Wenger understands identity as a learning trajectory, as a 'work in progress' and Paechter argues that identities can also be locational, so that new identities are developed as individuals move from one institution to another. When children joined the Nursery class or moved into Reception they wanted to be accepted into a community of masculinity or femininity. So they learned to adapt their behaviour according to what they perceived to be correct in different situations. They developed their identities as either a girl or a boy in relation to the norms of gendered behaviour they encountered.

Spaces and activities for girls

Girls in the early years classes played predominantly with other girls. They used an extensive range of communication strategies to show friendship and solidarity, talking about clothes, shoes, family, and Disney princess films, sharing jokes and pleasure in collaborative domestic play. They developed close friendships with each other through shared practices (George, 2007) such as greeting each other, physical closeness, shared gestures, sitting and talking together, doing helpful tasks in the classroom, and cooperative play centred on family roleplays, writing and drawing, and sand and water play. This fieldnote records how Nina and Madia chose to be together in Nursery:

> Nina comes in late, when children already on carpet. She looks for Madia, catches her eye, waves to her, Madia waves to back across carpet, and indicates that she should sit by her. They sit close, whisper and giggle together, are reprimanded by teacher. When told to go and choose an activity, they go together to the roleplay area.

Overtures and bids for friendship often took place when girls were doing activities they had chosen for themselves. Below, Zuhre and Yomi have chosen to do collage. Collage was chosen almost exclusively by girls, who enjoyed the activity and the social interaction.

> Zuhre doing collage. Yomi leaves Ayo at the water tray and comes and sits beside Zuhre, and begins a collage of her own.
>
> Yomi (smiling, making eye contact): 'It my dad's birthday today. You can come to my birthday too.'
>
> Zuhre (smiling, leaning towards Yomi): 'You can come to my birthday too.'

Girls claimed and developed friendships through repetitive exchanges like this, often with smiles and exchanges of eye contact. The interactions often had overtones of competition and power struggles. In the episode above, Yomi has quarrelled with Ayo and comes to sit with Zuhre, and Ayo can over-hear Yomi inviting Zuhre to her birthday.

In the next episode, Madia takes on the role of instructor and shows Madison how to use a funnel. She is also positioning herself as more competent and powerful than Madison.

> Madia and Madison in cooperative play at water tray.
>
> Madia: 'Watch me!'
>
> Madison: 'Look, quick!' (water spills)
>
> Madia: 'Oh Madison!' (Madia holds bottle, Madison pours.)
>
> Madison: 'I make it bigger for you.'
>
> Madia: 'Here, Madison, what you doing again Madison?' (in pleasant jokey re-buking tone).
>
> Madison is trying to pour water with the funnel upside down. Madia demon-strates how to do it properly, Madison holding the bottle, Madia pouring through funnel.

Girls frequently assumed a role of being helpful, sometimes taking on a quasi-teacher role with other children, especially younger ones. Older girls demonstrated to younger girls their knowledge of classroom routines and skills such as the ability to write their names.

> Ayo brings Molly to writing area, finds and shows her her name label, helps her write her name by giving instructions.
>
> Ayo: 'Molly, let's do a rainbow. I have a bad cold today. Molly, why did you do this?' (critical 'teacher' voice) 'Molly, let me do it for you. It's supposed to be like this.' (Ayo's tone is kind, helpful, slightly patronising, showing off her superior skills).

Here Ayo is initiating Molly into schoolgirl community of practice, encouraging Molly to be an apprentice. Molly tries to do what Ayo tells her, looks serious, but does not say much. Later that afternoon I saw them playing together outside in the Playhouse, laughing and giving each other lots of hugs and eye contact.

Spaces and activities for boys

Boys in Ash Vale early years classes chose each other as playmates and enjoyed demonstrating that they took part in activities that were marked for boys. The boys learned to take part in superhero play and battles, football and construction (including Lego, train and car play). Boys usually avoided physical contact with girls. Boys dominated activities in construction areas, play with vehicles, and ball games. They rarely chose collage or writing activities. Many took pleasure in demonstrating physical strength, ball skills, ability to build elaborate constructions, and engaged in fighting games including rescue operations, animal and pirate battles.

Boys sometimes used words, gestures and bodily postures to exclude girls from areas and activities usually dominated by boys. Below, a group of girls play together, unusually, in the Nursery construction area but are soon ousted by a boy, Kumi.

> 1.10 Kumi, Chloe, Sara, Sammie go to big bricks on construction mat.
>
> Sammie, Sara and Chloe go on building their house, and resume the domestic roleplay that they started earlier.
>
> ...
>
> Kumi making long tower with bricks, uses it like a sabre, 'piu' 'wop' 'woah' lots of thrusting and waving it around, taking up most of the space.

1.11 Sammie: 'I gonna do something else.'

Goes to roleplay area. Chloe follows her, they start a game in there with dolls.

Sara goes on making house, quite elaborate by now, has 3 play people.

Kumi waves his tower at Sara, (and at Tagan and Lan at collage table) 'SSSS a snake!'

1.14 Sara leaves area, goes to roleplay area, leaving Kumi on own.

Kumi to BM: 'Look at this!'

BM: 'What is it Kumi?'

Kumi: 'A machine' (shows me the two parts and how they can be pressed down to work it).

BM: 'What does it do?'

Kumi: 'It a gun.' (challengingly, looks at me, like, what do you say to that, expects me to object?)

BM: 'Oh, I see.'

(I notice he has 'accidently' knocked down the girls' house with his legs).

It took six minutes for Kumi to get the area to himself. He has not spoken to any of the girls or directly threatened them physically; he has just taken up a lot of space and introduced a different kind of discourse, a fighting game. I have colluded in this by failing to intervene when he started waving his sabre and making his war noises, then endorsing his choice of construction by asking him questions about it, and not pointing out that he has destroyed the girls' house. The girls move their play to the roleplay area, but they have far less space in there as it is much smaller than the construction area, and they have no bricks.

This episode shows how some older boys learned to take for granted their right to occupy the space in the construction area. Domination of areas of the Nursery class and Garden was an important aspect of becoming a member of the boys' community of practice of masculinity. Younger boys saw established Nursery boys regularly taking equipment and space from girls, and modelled their own behaviour on what they saw. Adults in the setting unwittingly endorsed this behaviour by not challenging it. My own conversation with Kumi in the above episode probably reinforced his assumption that the construction space belonged to him, as a boy. I often saw boys barging into girls, pushing them out of the way, and casually poking them. The girls seldom protested, or only mildly.

Jake and Nina at puzzle table.

Jake pokes Nina quite hard. (I can see no provocation from Nina, who is getting on with her own puzzle. She does not react).

Some boys used physical gestures and noises to exclude girls from activities in boys' spaces. In the following episode, Madia tries to play with the cars on the construction mat.

Reece, Femi, Harrison and Madia on carpet with cars.

Harrison (loudly): 'Madia isn't sharing the cars.'

Boys ignore Madia, make comments only to each other.

... Omar joins car play – very confidently.

Reece to Omar (pleasant voice, one mate to another): 'Don't break it that's an aeroplane.'

Omar (nods to him): 'Neow' flying the plane. Parallel play.

Omar is readily accepted into the vehicle play, in contrast to Madia.

Madia (frozen look on her face) tries to collect and hold on to some cars, but goes to the water tray after three minutes.

Harrison accuses Madia of not sharing the cars, but it would seem that the boys do not want her on the construction mat with them. She has an unpleasant experience there, and it may well put her off going there again. I recorded her subsequently going to the collage table, roleplay area and water tray but not the construction area. Through experiences such as this, girls learn that certain areas in the Nursery are not for them.

Making guns for battle play was a major practice of masculinity in Reception. Some boys were aggressive towards girls, not only by taking up space but also by threatening girls with physical gestures. In the play episode below, Ben makes a gun, and Jala tells him this is not responsible and threatens to tell the teacher, so he pretends it is something else. When Ben menaces her with his gun Jala can experience a moment of power by taking up a sensible good girl role.

Construction area

Jala (only girl) Ben, Jake, Femi

Ben: 'I'm making a gun.' (with stickle bricks, points it at Jala and makes firing sounds).

Jala: 'No! You not allowed to make a gun. You gotta be responsible. That's not responsible.' (said in an adult tone).

33

Jala gets up, as if to go and tell teacher.

Ben: (quickly, urgent voice): 'No. I not making a gun. It something else.'

Jala comes back, sits down.

Here Jala is learning to position herself as a sensible girl and this is frequently the only way girls can experience power in classrooms where boys control space and resources and harass girls.

> Of the feminine construction, maturity, obedience and neatness are the valued 'sensible' qualities, which naturally lead to 'selflessness' – giving and facilitating. The masculine construction involves 'silly' qualities of immaturity, messiness and naughtiness, leading to 'selfishness' – taking and demanding. (Francis, 1998:40)

I found that these constructs had an impact on gendered power relations as girls sought recognition and praise for positioning themselves as sensible in opposition to boys' enactment of silly. The construction of boys as irresponsible enabled some boys to dominate space and resources. Young children's constructs of masculinity and femininity are embedded in dualistic gender discourses, and their rigid views of appropriate behaviours for boys and girls are often attempts to reduce uncertainties and position themselves successfully (Browne, 2004).

When boys and girls played together they took part in complicated negotiations and made compromises. We see this clearly with Ayo and Harrison in the following tea party episode at the water tray in the Nursery. I include a detailed analysis of this episode because it demonstrates the complexities of power relationships between boys and girls and shows how children reworked and refined gender discourses through their play.

At the beginning of this episode at the water tray, Ayo and Yomi try to establish it as a girls only activity. Harrison persists in joining in the action, listing boys in the Nursery class in his support, although they are not physically present at the water tray. When Yomi splashes him, he appeals to Mrs Jones and when Yomi has gone he holds his own with Ayo. Harrison positions himself as instructor to Femi in the masculine domain of the construction area, thus securely within membership of the boys' community of practice, but he combines this with more experimental play with Ayo at the water tray.

> Ayo moves to the water tray (loudly):'Let's make a tea party'
>
> Yomi joins her. Harrison joins after two minutes.
>
> Ayo: 'This for girls.'

34

Yomi: 'This is for girls team.'

Harrison: 'This for boys team. Ravi, Jake, Reece, Kumi , Omar'

Yomi: '??? (inaudible)'

Harrison: 'You not allowed to do that. My Mum says you not allowed call me names.'

Yomi: (ignores him:)'...I'm so strong. Did you watch Jackanory Ayo?'

Ayo: 'Yeah'

Harrison: 'I watched it too.'

Ayo: 'Let's make this tea party again.'

Yomi splashes Harrison. Harrison complains to Mrs Jones.

Mrs Jones: 'I'm very disappointed in you Yomi. Take off your apron and go and draw a picture for Harrison to say sorry to him.'

Yomi gives Harrison a hostile look, then goes to the other end of the room.

Ayo: 'Thanks Harrison!' (scathingly, as in what did you have to tell the teacher for?)

Harrison: 'I gonna say to my brother' (splashes Ayo).

Ayo: 'Mrs Jones, he wet me.'

Mrs Jones (mildly):'Be careful with the water. Maybe you should move round a bit Ayo.'

Yomi and Harrison both splashed water. Mrs Jones dealt more severely with Yomi, perhaps because Yomi was seen as a troublemaker. She was beginning to have a reputation as a naughty girl, partly because she was assertive.

Ayo to Harrison (taking the teapot): 'I had that! Harrison, you just have to put more water in there.'

Harrison (indicating cup of water):'You have to pretend to be drinking it.'

Ayo (primly): 'You're not allowed to drink it.'

Harrison (sounding cross, as if, you are deliberately misunderstanding me): 'No, you have to pretend.'

Ayo (firmly): 'Harrison, can you put the drink there?' (ie in the teapot)

Harrison: 'No.'

Ayo (indicating side of tray next to her): 'Put it in there.'

Harrison (irritated voice): 'Ayo, I put it in there. I gonna put it back in there.'

Ayo asserts herself as the one who is making the decisions and up to this point Harrison accepted this, though not without protest. A tea party usually happened in the roleplay area, dominated by girls. Here, Harrison is enjoying the opportunity to take part in roleplay. When Femi joins the play, Ayo and Harrison cooperate to bring him into line and keep the tea party going.

Harrison to Femi: 'We're making a tea party.'

Ayo: 'Harrison is right.'

Femi stirs spoon in cups vigorously.

Ayo: 'I was in Tesco. My Mum taked me.' To Harrison 'Can you get that for me Harrison?'

Harrison passes cup to her.

Femi: 'This is magic' (vigorously churning the water around).

Harrison to Femi: 'No Femi! Femi is spoiling the party.'

Ayo (charmingly): 'Beautiful tea!'

Harrison: 'We making a tea party ain't it Ayo?'

Femi takes off his apron, goes to car mat.

...

Harrison takes off his apron goes to join Femi on car mat.

Harrison: 'On your marks, get set, Yeah!'

Femi: 'Yum, vum, vum!'

Harrison (in a 'teacher' voice): 'You have to check, then go.'

9.45 Ayo alone at water tray. To Harrison: 'Harrison, come back!'

Harrison leaves cars and returns to water tray.

Ayo (gives him a cup of water):'Here's tea and I put sugar'

Harrison (pretending to drink): 'It's delicious!'

Ayo (Harrison drops a cup on floor): 'Oh, my goodness!' (sounding like an exasperated Mother/teacher)

9.50 Harrison wipes hands, returns to car mat.

Ayo: 'Harrison, come back!'

Harrison: 'No, I'm *have* to be here for Femi.'

Harrison to Femi (firmly): 'You have to do the traffic. Peep, peep.'

Femi: 'Peep, peep.'

Harrison: 'You have to use another car.' (Harrison is now taking the role of instructor, telling Femi what to do with the cars.)

Femi:'My Dad's 18 years old.'

Harrison: 'My Dad's 91'

Femi (sounds impressed): 'Woah!'

Harrison: 'What's your Mum?'

Femi:'My Mum's 18'

Harrison: 'That's a small number.'

9.55 Harrison returns to watertray.

Ayo (to Harrison): 'You've been a long time with Femi'.

Ayo (to Femi): Are you goin to come and have a tea party with us Femi?' (Ayo tries to get Femi to join her tea party game).

(No response from Femi, who goes on playing with cars).

Ayo enjoys organising the tea party, dominating the play at the water tray for over half an hour. Twice, she asks Harrison to leave the car mat to play with her. Harrison enjoys the tea party game with her so much that he returns to it twice and he takes an active part in the imaginative dialogue. But he makes Ayo wait, taking time on the construction mat with Femi. He shows Femi how to play with cars in the construction area, and this is one of the key practices of masculinity in the Nursery. He tells Ayo:

'No, I'm *have* to be here for Femi.'

This remark suggests that he sees his role as instructor and guide for Femi as a matter of duty rather than pleasure. Ayo has just scolded him for dropping a cup, so he might also be punishing her by withdrawing. He enjoys instructing Femi on how to play on the car mat, but also enjoys the tea party play with Ayo. This is an interesting episode, because it is unusual for a girl and boy to play together for such a long time in this Nursery. The water tray was not seen by the children as either for boys or for girls. It was relatively gender neutral territory and therefore had the potential for girls and boys to explore and develop their relationships together.

Discussion
Read the water tray episode again. In what ways do
     Ayo

Harrison

Mrs Jones

draw on discourses of gender dualism?

How do Mrs Jones' interventions affect the children's play?

Can you think how early years educators could have helped the children in this episode play together in non-gender stereotyped ways?

Reinforcing gender dualism

Staff assumptions about gender differences often reinforced gender dualism in Ash Vale. Staff expected boys and girls would work together when given tasks in class, but would play in same-sex groups in different spaces when given a choice.

> BM to Mrs Daly: ' I am looking to see where girls and boys play together'.
>
> Mrs Daly (classroom assistant): 'They don't play together much... It is always female dominated in the playhouse'

Blaise (2005) shows how one girl in her research Nursery, who is assertive and keen to do construction activities, became a leader in encouraging other girls to do construction, and how the teacher allowed girls to reserve time in the construction area. The teacher's awareness and support was crucial to the girls' successful border crossing. In contrast, staff in my research classes seemed to think it was natural for boys to dominate the construction areas so did not intervene to support the girls' efforts to gain access. When I talked with the classroom assistant, Ms Kent told me:

> I don't notice who chooses what. I am just looking to see that everybody is behaving properly and doing what they should be. The boys go to the construction, that's what they like to do.

This remark is not as contradictory as it first appears, as Ms Kent is reiterating a version of the tenets of *developmentally appropriate practice*. She maintains that children should be given free choice in play opportunities, but this ignores the problem that many of the children themselves think they should take part in gender marked activities.

Lloyd and Duveen (1992) show how teachers often use gender as a social category, which contributes to children's gender marking of activities and behaviour. Educators give mixed messages to children by saying, for example,

38

'We don't have girls' only tables,' but at the same time, saying 'Boys, stop shouting!' Browne's research in early years classes in the UK (2004) shows how educators describe boys and girls in binary terms: boys are 'physical, competitive and noisy' and girls 'chatty, calm and attentive, eager to please.' Ofsted's Report on the Foundation Stage (2007) uses similar dualistic descriptions.

Staff in Ash Vale expected boys and girls to play at separate activities because they believe girls and boys are innately different. These beliefs stem from discourses of developmental psychology and long-established early years educational practice. Early childhood pedagogy is strongly influenced by theories from developmental psychology. I set these in their historical context, as some will be challenged here (MacNaughton, 2000; Robinson and Jones Diaz, 2006).

Modern British developmental psychology became established during the late 19th century to tackle questions related to evolutionary theory, anthropology and philosophy. A hierarchical concept of development was presupposed, and a normal path of human development based on biological principles was assumed. Most 19th and 20th century research into young children was dominated by approaches taken from natural sciences. Children were seen as in the process of becoming adults, progressing through observable stages of adaptation to the environment.

Children were seen by 19th century western scientists in a similar light to 'primitive peoples': as intellectually immature. They were studied through observational methods that claimed to be objective and privileged rationality, which was seen as a masculine attribute. These scientific discourses were used to promote political agendas that perpetuated and attempted to justify inequalities and oppression based on class, race and gender (Robinson and Jones Diaz, 2006). For example, gendered practices of scientific research into children's development excluded women and mothers on grounds that they were too emotional and insufficiently objective to investigate children's patterns of behaviour (Burman, 1994).

The establishment in the late 19th century of clinics and nursery schools where large numbers of children could be observed and measured, facilitated the growth of developmental psychology (Burman, 1994). Controlled experiments allowed researchers to use standardisation and analysis to construct norms based on average performance of children in tests and examinations at certain ages. These results were then used to assess other children, comparing them to the established norms. Research in developmental psychology sought to understand how the individual child develops through a sequence of stages of which the highest is the use of abstract reasoning.

> Developmental psychology is wholly predicated on the notion of childhood's 'naturalness' and on the necessity, normality and desirability of development and constructive change through 'growth'. Children are thus routinely constructed as partially rational – that is, in the process of becoming rational. (Jenks, 2004:79)

This developmental discourse of childhood sees childhood as a preparation for adulthood (Walkerdine, 2004). Theories from developmental psychology are used to establish norms which lay claim to universal application.

> Although most of these theories have been developed from limited populations, often white and male, they are expected to apply to all. Those who do not follow the appropriate path are treated as problems, not for the theory, but for themselves and /or society; their trajectories are seen as pathological. (Paechter, 1998:58)

Piaget's theories were hugely influential. In his stages of development (1977), the child is an egocentric individual progressing through measurable stages of age-related cognitive development. Piaget's child is supposedly gender-neutral, but actually has stereotypical masculine attributes, such as playfulness, creativity and rule-breaking (Walkerdine, 1988, 2004).

Child-centred pedagogy drew on Piaget's work, arguing that a child's learning takes place through individual discovery. Theories from developmental psychology were adopted as the central principles of western early childhood education, enshrined in developmentally appropriate practice (DAP) (MacNaughton, 2000). The child is seen as naturally progressing through defined stages of development.

In this scenario, the task of the (usually female) teacher is to foster and nurture this natural development, by providing appropriately stimulating play experiences to enable the child to progress through the stages. The teacher is required to engage in constant observation of each child so she can provide for his cognitive and emotional needs. The child-centred discourse has a model of a male child as an active learner, engaged in free experimentation and discovery, with the (female) teacher positioned as attentive and nurturing, at risk of harming the natural development of her charges if she fails to facilitate their progress (Paechter, 1998).

Piaget's hierarchy of cognitive progression is, however, an inadequate explanation of children's emotional and social development. Subsequent psychological theory and research explored children's understanding of social relationships and demonstrated that, from infancy, children engage in meaning-making and engage with the emotions and behaviour of others as active social players (Dunn, 1998; Trevarthen, 1998). Donaldson (1978) demonstrated that Piaget failed to take full account of the importance of context in assessing children's thinking, and that children as young as three appreciate others' viewpoints and reason deductively.

Vygotsky (1978) showed that behaviour is culturally contextualised, learned through adult scaffolding and modelling, with children as active participants. Bruner (1986) argued that the scaffolding of early adult-child interaction begins through adults attributing intentional communication to young children. And Rogoff (1990) demonstrated that children learn within specific social contexts, through guided participation in cultural activities.

Yet although the limitations of Piagetian theories have been exposed, the discourse of developmentally appropriate practice continues to underpin western early childhood pedagogy (Grieshaber and Cannella, 2001). The term DAP, formalised in the USA with the publication of the National Association for the Education of Young Children's booklet on Developmentally Appropriate Practice (DAP) (Bredekamp, 1987), enshrined Piaget's principles of using individual play as a central means of encouraging children's learning. The teacher's role was to be a provider of appropriate materials and concrete experiences to enable children to progress through developmental stages by self-directed experimentation. Teachers were encouraged to undertake ongoing observations of individual children, with the goal of providing age and stage appropriate experiences. These principles were adopted as central tenets of early childhood education in Australia and the UK. Using Piaget as a guide to good practice made adult intervention in children's learning problematic, and gave no framework for examining children's power relations.

Schools continue to function as sites for the production of a certain kind of unitary, rational subject (Walkerdine, 1999). Child development knowledge and DAP have become a regime of truth that regulates and governs the organisation of young children's learning. Developmental truths are cited to normalise, classify and regulate children in early years settings, and it is difficult for early years educators to challenge DAP (Blaise, 2005; MacNaughton, 2005). Staff in Ash Vale adhered firmly to DAP principles, and this poses problems for gender equity work. If we think we should not intervene in children's free play we cannot help them explore alternative gender positions, nor see the power relationships that often underpin their actions.

Reconceptualists in early years education have challenged DAP principles. They argue that DAP has contributed to social inequality and injustice by ignoring sexism, racism and issues of (dis)ability, class and sexuality (Robinson and Jones Diaz, 2006). Some reconceptualists, including Cannella (1997), argue that DAP institutionalises white, male, middle class systems of morality, with class-based and differentiated curriculum goals, privileging a monocultural approach and ignoring issues of social justice. Reconceptualists point out that working class children are labelled as deficient and their home backgrounds as inadequate because they have different cultural norms. As MacNaughton maintains, attempts to impose so-called universal norms amount to violence:

> Early childhood educators who reproduce and act on these supposedly universal developmental norms are committing a form of violence that privileges cultural homogeneity and marginalises cultural diversity. (MacNaughton, 2005: 37)

Within discourses of developmentally appropriate practice in contemporary English education, children's development is controlled through the teaching of the National Curriculum. DAP discourses operate alongside a discourse that sees early childhood education as a time of training and preparation for formal schooling and the serious adult world of work. Children are taught to use their minds and bodies in specific ways, often privileging cognitive over emotional development (Burman, 1994). The Foundation Stage goals emphasise the development of rational thought, independence and formal skills. Educators are expected to intervene to regulate children's behaviour to ensure that these goals are met.

DAP discourses emphasise the importance of child-centred learning contexts, whereby individual children are encouraged to explore materials independently and develop concepts through free play and discovery. The principles of DAP are often given as reasons for non-intervention in children's free play. The emphasis on allowing children to engage in free play means that issues of social justice are often marginalised in early years practice. As MacNaughton urges (2000), practitioners need to ask what children in their setting are free to do, which children are able to make choices, and who is excluded from various activities. The next chapters explore the choices available to children in early years classes at Ash Vale.

Key themes

Three major themes which run throughout the book are summarised below.

Space, power and knowledge

Children's use of play spaces and choice of play activities is directly related to gendered power and knowledge relations. Power relations between children are important in shaping their play. Some children learn to dominate particular spaces by claiming them for boys or for girls. Children police play activities strictly, insisting that certain activities are for girls or for boys. Older boys and girls use what they know about masculine and feminine activities to dominate other children and seize moments of power.

Apprentice participation

New pupils learn from older children how to be apprentices in play that emphasises gender differences.

Gender borderwork

Children are involved in gender borderwork, frequently policing gender boundaries to keep boys and girls separate. However, children do sometimes attempt to cross gender boundaries in their play.

See also Glossary p135.

Recommended reading

Browne, N (2004) *Gender Equity in the Early Years.* Maidenhead: Open University Press

MacNaughton, G (2000) *Rethinking Gender in Early Childhood Education.* London: Sage Publications

MacNaughton, G (2005) *Doing Foucault in Early Childhood Studies.* London: Routledge

Paechter, C (2007) *Being Boys, Being Girls: Learning masculinities and femininities.* Maidenhead: Open University Press

Thorne, B. (1993) *Gender Play: Girls and boys in school.* Buckingham: Open University Press

Weedon, C (1987) *Feminist Practice and Poststructuralist Theory.* Oxford: Basil Blackwell

Yelland, N (ed) (1998) *Gender in Early Childhood.* London: Routledge

3

Outdoor Play: 'Skipping is for girls' and 'football is for boys'?

Girls taking turns jumping over rope.
Marsha starts chant: 'Ole, Ole, Ole,' as they jump.
3 boys with hoods up, attacking mode, dash right into the skipping rope.
Lisa shouts: 'You move out of the way!'
Boys laugh and run on across playground to join a football game.

This is a typical example of lunchtime play in Ash Vale Reception playground. Boys frequently disrupted girls' skipping games. The largest space in the playground was dominated by boys playing football. Girls seldom played. Children who were new in Ash Vale learned from established children that 'football is for boys' and 'skipping is for girls'. This chapter explores how children learned these gendered behaviours.

Skipping ropes and football – using play technologies

Children in Ash Vale early years classes learned from each other how to use the play technologies of skipping ropes and footballs. Lave and Wenger (1991) use the term 'technologies' to describe how newcomers have to learn how to use tools to become members of communities of practice. Just as apprentice butchers have to learn to use knives and cleavers, children new to Ash Vale learned from others how to use play objects such as footballs and skipping ropes. The children applied knowledge and skills to particular ways of using play objects – or *play technologies*. They learned to play with these objects in gendered ways: girls became members of a community of practice of femininity by playing with skipping ropes; boys joined a community of practice of masculinity by playing football.

Two interrelated processes were involved in the development of these communities of practice. Children learned to play in ways that became important to their sense of self through shared play activities (Wenger, 1998; Paechter, 2007). At the same time, the communities were in a process of constant reconstruction, change and development, as new members learned to participate and meanings were negotiated and reworked. The communities of practice of girls and boys were not static or fixed and there were conflicts between continuity and displacement, demonstrated in power struggles, for example when newcomers moved from peripheral to full participation. Children had different interests and made different contributions. But they learned to demonstrate shared understandings about what it meant to be a boy or a girl in these playground games.

Gendered power and knowledge relations were sustained, re-enacted, reworked and sometimes challenged through the ways the children used skipping ropes and footballs. To become full members of communities of practice of femininity and masculinity the new girls and boys had to learn the skills and appropriate uses of these play technologies. The girls wanted to learn skipping and the boys wanted to learn football, not just so they could demonstrate their skills but also because they could then become part of the boys' or girls' playground communities. Their sense of personal identity became bound up with playing these games, since

> ...understanding the technology of practice is more than learning to use the tools; it is a way to connect with the history of the practice and to participate more directly in its cultural life. (Lave and Wenger, 1991:101)

Historical and cultural connections can be seen in the ways the children learned to use skipping ropes and footballs. Girls learned how to use skipping ropes in specific ways through peripheral participation in the games of older girls, connecting with the history of skipping games through rhymes and shared practices. Boys learned to use footballs through peripheral participation in the games of older boys, connecting to the wider history of men's football through knowledge of the game, and cultural associations, such as wearing football team shirts. Boys seized opportunities to demonstrate their football skills and girls to show their skipping skills.

The use of play technologies of skipping ropes and footballs is linked to processes of *reification*, as Wenger calls the process by which certain objects and practices are taken as markers of community membership or points of focus for organising the negotiation of meanings within communities of practice (Wenger, 1998:59). It has been widely documented how boys often use knowledge and expertise about sport as a way of defining their community, and actively exclude girls, even when girls display knowledge and skills (Nespor, 1997; Swain, 2003; Blaise, 2005; Paechter, 2007). In Ash Vale some objects and practices associated with skipping and football became reified as markers of masculinity and femininity in particular contexts. These markers were deeply embedded in children's power relations.

Below I discuss how new girls learned that skipping is for girls and new boys learned that football is for boys through legitimate peripheral apprentice participation in the games of more established classmates. The children learned social rules about how to perform masculinities and femininities through gendered uses of play objects.

'Skipping is for girls'

Children gradually learned that skipping was a shared activity for girls in Ash Vale early years classes. When children were in the Nursery, ropes were freely available as play objects outside in the Garden. Girls and boys sometimes played with skipping ropes, and some children began to experiment with trying to jump over them. One child held onto the ends of a short rope and tried to jump over it, or two children held a long rope and turned it so that another child could jump over it. The Nursery staff said they had not seen a child who could skip properly at the age of 3 or 4, although young children often enjoyed trying to. I saw boys and girls having a go at conventional skipping with ropes. However, I usually saw children in Nursery using the ropes for other games, such as chasing, monster games and as reins for imaginary horses and for tying up people in prisoner and rescue operations. Girls and boys in Nursery were already using ropes in different ways, although there was some overlap at this age.

The following fieldnote shows the use of a skipping rope during a Nursery playtime, and is typical of how ropes were used in Ash Vale Nursery. Two girls, Oni and Tagan use a long skipping rope in the conventional girls' way, and they allow Oni's younger brother Ade to join in. Oni is not yet skilled at turning the rope, and accidentally hurts a younger girl, Nina. One of the younger boys, Ervin, has a brief go with the rope and another boy, Omar, uses it as a whip in his riding game.

> Oni and Tagan turning big skipping rope together. Nina watching.
>
> Ade jumps in the rope.
>
> Tagan drops the rope.

Nina jumps in.

Lots of giggles.

Tagan and Oni turn rope very quickly, Oni lets go of it and accidentally the handle catches Nina and hurts her.

Nina starts to cry and goes inside.

...

Ervin picks up the rope, makes skipping like movements then drops it on ground.

...

Omar gets hold of the rope, running round the play area with it, holding on to one end, making whipping motions.

Omar: 'Ya, ya, go, go, go!'

Boys in the Reception playground used skipping ropes in different ways to the girls. Girls almost always used them for organised skipping games, often helped by dinner staff or Year 6 girls. Two girls turned the rope, and the others took it in turns to jump in it, joining in with counting and rhymes. The older girls dominated these skipping games, showing the younger ones what to do. Sometimes there were arguments over whose turn it was, or whether somebody was out. These skipping games took place at one end of the Reception playground, and the only rule for joining in was that you had to be a girl.

When I asked the Reception girls about skipping games, they all confirmed that it was a game for girls, and that boys did not play. Below, Nadia explains that she does not play skipping with Charlie because he is can't skip – presumably because he is a boy. She therefore plays basketball with him. Interestingly, basketball seemed to be an acceptable game for boys and girls to play together. The children all had a go at skipping in PE lessons, but boys did not get as much practice as the girls and tended to be less enthusiastic and less skilled. And they got no chance to learn the skipping rhymes from the older girls.

Interview with Nadia, Molly, Shona

Nadia: 'I like to play with Molly and Ayla. Skipping rope.'

...

BM: 'Do you like to play with any boys.?'

Nadia nods.

Lan's picture of herself skipping with her girlfriends

BM: 'Who?'

Nadia: 'Charlie.'

BM: 'What do you play with Charlie?'

Nadia: 'He can't do skipping.'

BM: 'Would you let him play skipping with you if he wanted to?'

Nadia: 'Basketball. I play basketball with Charlie, not skipping, cos he can't do it.'

In the next interview Lan tells me a skipping rhyme and goes on to draw a wonderful picture of herself and her girlfriends skipping together. Clearly she gets much pleasure from both the social and physical aspects of skipping, and this group identity shows in her drawing. Lan portrays herself and her friends in stylised girlie dresses like those worn by Barbie princesses, with long hair and identical big smiles. In fact Lan is Vietnamese and has short straight hair and her friends were from several ethnic groups. None looked like a Barbie princess. Nevertheless, Lan's wonderful picture conveys that her favourite playtime activity was belonging to a group of girls who skipped together. Other Reception girls, too, told me it was their favourite thing.

Lan: 'I like to play skipping with Zuhre and Chloe and Sara. I like to jump in the big rope. We do apple pie.'

BM: 'Apple Pie? How does that go?'

> Lan: 'Apple crumble
>
> Apple pie
>
> Tell me the name
>
> Of your sweetie pie
>
> ABCDE (etc through the alphabet).
>
> Then you say the name of sweetie pie.'

As well as skipping in the big rope, the girls also skipped with individual ropes, often in pairs. It seemed virtually the only game some of the girls played that was energetic. Hide and seek and chasing games were popular with some girls, but others seemed reluctant to run around. They said running was against the rules, or that they were afraid of falling over. Some girls wore shoes that were unsuitable for active play and this might have contributed to their lack of confidence. Running in the Nursery garden was forbidden, although most boys ignored this rule. Some girls told me it was a rule in the Reception playground, although it was not.

Younger girls learned the rhymes from older girls. The rhymes often involved repetition of heterosexualised scripts. As Epstein argues, the rhymes are 'certainly reproducing part of a culture of heterosexuality in which girls grow up to be women who marry men, go on honeymoon, and have babies' (Epstein, 1997:43). In one popular rhyme on the theme of marriage and babies, the girls inserted the names of boys they knew. This was sometimes done to tease boys who had disrupted their game.

> (Jason had been running across the skipping rope earlier)
>
> Ayla, Lan, Molly skipping
>
> Lan: 'Jason Jason, will you marry me,
>
> How many children will we see? (repeats this chant three times).

As Thorne shows, episodes where girls seize power take place in the context of girls' daily experience of playground aggression from certain boys. Boys' harassment of girls often takes the same form as sexual harassment.

> The harasser, nearly always male, often claims that verbal and physical intrusions into the target's personal space are 'all in fun', while the target, usually female, sees it as unwanted and even coercive attention. (Thorne, 1993:80)

Reception boys did play with ropes, but not for skipping. They used them for tug-of-war, strangling and fighting, and for capture and rescue games. Girls very occasionally joined in. I often saw boys disrupting skipping games.

These took up a small area of the Reception playground, compared to boys' football games. It seemed that wherever the girls put their skipping rope, boys would run into it. In the next episode, Jake deliberately takes hold of the rope to prevent the girls from skipping.

> Chloe turning rope on left, Sara on right. Marsha, Molly, Zuhre waiting by wall for turn.
>
> Lan and Shona jumping in.
>
> Jake comes over to wall.
>
> Jake takes the rope, makes whipping motions with it.
>
> Outcry from girls. Game disintegrates. Rope lies on ground, abandoned.

In the following play episode Marsha seizes power by using a popular skipping chant to make fun of Jake for disrupting the girls' skipping game.

> *Reception playground*
>
> Marsha taking lead in organising skipping game now.
>
> Girls chanting loudly: 'Tell me the name of your sweetheart, ABCDE....
>
> Jake runs into the rope, laughing.
>
> Marsha (to dinner supervisor): 'Miss, he's spoilt it!'
>
> Dinner supervisor intervenes, tells Jake to move away.
>
> Jake moves away, still within earshot.
>
> Marsha (loudly chanting): 'Tell me the name of your sweetheart. JAKE! Jake!'
>
> Girls scream and laugh.
>
> Girls chanting together: 'Jake! Jake!'
>
> Jake looks uncomfortable, moves further away.

The girls took a small area of the playground for their skipping game, and even this area was contested by some of the boys. In the play episode described we see a group of girls acting together to seize power, albeit briefly, using the heterosexual skipping chant and shared laughter to discomfort Jake, who had been harassing them. Opportunities to resist *hegemonic* power relations can emerge through practices that 'work the weakness in the norm' (Butler, 2004), as illustrated in this play episode.

Butler (1993) argues that a child is gendered at birth by being named girl or boy, depending on the presence or absence of a penis, and can only be understood as properly human if designated one or the other. She argues that the initiatory performative 'It's a girl' means that she must learn to embody certain ideals of femininity, in order to qualify as a fully human subject. Butler shows how femininities and masculinities are constructed in relation to heterosexuality.

> Gender norms operate by requiring the embodiment of certain ideals of femininity and masculinity, ones that are almost all related to the idealization of the heterosexual bond ... Femininity is thus not the product of a choice, but the forcible citation of a norm, one whose complex historicity is indissociable from relations of discipline, regulation, punishment. (Butler, 1993:231/2)

Butler uses the term 'heterosexual matrix' to describe the way that gender is constructed, arguing that heterosexuality operates through the regulated production of exaggerated forms of 'man' and 'woman', requiring compulsory performances, but that heterosexual norms are 'haunted by their own in-efficacy' (Butler, 1990). Butler argues that heterosexual regimes never fully legislate or contain their own ideals, so they have potential for subversion. Therefore gender categories can be destabilised by 'working the weakness in the norm'.

Although clearly still operating within a framework of *heteronormativity*, Marsha takes the lead in encouraging the girls to position themselves briefly as powerful in relation to Jake. Butler (1990, 1993) shows how gender and heterosexuality are entwined and unstable, and how their 'normality' is upheld by the policing of Other sexualities and gender positions. Butler understands gender as a process, 'a set of repeated acts within a highly rigid regulatory frame' (Butler, 1990:33). Thus gender can be seen as a series of acts, not a thing, emphasising the way 'we do become what we practice being' (Frye, 1983:34). This is a useful way of conceptualising gender when doing research with children because it captures the way they experiment with gender positions.

Renold (2005) argues that discourses of innocent childhood construct young children as asexual, but that sexual innocence is just something adults would like to believe of children. Robinson and Jones Diaz (2006) show how the construction of heterosexuality and heterosexual desire are part of young children's everyday life, and note that this contradicts the presumption that young children are too young to understand sexuality. Epstein (1997) and Renold (2005) show how primary schools are key sites for the production of sexualities through the formal and informal curriculum and through children's informal sexual cultures.

Children use spaces in the playground and other school spaces to explore and police sexualities and display gendered sexual knowledge (Best, 1983; Thorne, 1993; Renold, 2005). As Renold (2005) points out, sexual practices vary between spaces, within and between schools and year groups, and shift over time. Most research on sexual cultures has focused on older children and adolescents but a number of early years researchers have explored young children's heterosexualised power relationships (Epstein, 1997; MacNaughton, 2000, 2005; Connolly, 2004; Blaise, 2005; Bhana, 2005). As Renold (2005) argues, girls and boys experience sexualisation in multiple and different ways, but all positions are produced within a heteronormative framework of compulsory *heterosexuality*.

Legitimate participation in play activities

I was particularly interested in exploring how children were included or excluded in gendered play, and how they policed their own behaviour and that of others. In the next play episode, in the Reception playground at lunch time, Sara tries to let a new boy join a skipping game, but Ayo and Marsha prevent it.

> New boy Leon from Nursery comes to where Sara is sitting, Sara gets up and gives him the rope to turn. He sits in the chair in which Sara had been sitting.
>
> Outcry from other girls.
>
> Ayo (very annoyed, loud, disgusted tone, emphasising 'white' and 'boy') 'That *white boy*, I don't know his name, he doesn't even know what to do!'
>
> Sara goes and sits by herself on bench by shed.
>
> Tussle whilst Ayo and Marsha try to wrench the rope from Leon's hands. They succeed in getting it from him. He gives up and goes to sit with Sara on bench by shed.

When Ayo talks about the boy who is trying to join the girls' skipping game, she is saying 'white boy' to describe him as an outsider. What she means is: 'he is not one of us, and he shouldn't be allowed to play this game because he does not belong, and he will spoil it for us'. She has experience of what boys like him do, boys like Jake in her class. Ayo says 'white boy' in disparaging tones, and says she does not know his name. Leon is new in the playground, and does not know the rules. He could possibly be incorporated into the game, but Ayo's sense of herself as a member of the community of practice of Reception girls does not, in this instance, encompass a play relationship with this outsider. She is outraged by his behaviour.

Ayo and Sara position themselves in different ways. Sara is prepared to let him have a turn and tries to make it possible for him to join in. Sara often border crossed successfully and she draws on discourses of fair play and equal opportunities. She told me she thinks boys and girls should be allowed to play with whatever they like. But she was unable to help Leon gain access to skipping. This episode shows how children work on their understanding of the salience of gender and ethnicity through their play, developing their own gender identities through relationships with others.

Football for boys – hegemonic masculinity at work

Some boys played boisterous football games at lunch play in Reception and in the Nursery garden. The boys' games dominated the play spaces. There was no marked out pitch for football in the Nursery, Reception or Year 1 play-grounds. In the Nursery garden, one end was used by boys for football games, with the entrance gate as a goal. The official rule of no running seemed to be ignored by boys and staff alike when football was in progress, although staff did sometimes tell boys not to run in the Nursery garden. Although the games were informal, the older boys in Nursery displayed considerable knowledge of the rules and behaviour, and practiced skills of dribbling, passing and scor-ing. They occasionally allowed younger boys to join in, if they were persistent.

Daniel, Jake, Ben, Ryan, Lewis, playing football, using gate as a goal.

Daniel: 'Yeah!' (adult footballer behaviour, running around, arms up, and cheer-ing)

Adil trying to join in football.

Lewis (to Adil): '*No!*'

Adil runs round football area for a while, trying to get to the ball, then runs over onto the slide.

...

Later that afternoon

Adil gets another big ball and is joining in with older boys now, trying to get his ball in goal.

In the next play episode, Daniel and Omar dominate the action, demonstrat-ing knowledge of football language, moves of the game, and how adult foot-ballers behave on the pitch.

Football game in Nursery garden, one ball, Omar, Daniel, Jake, Lewis.

Boys are trying to score goals against the gate.

Daniel to Omar: 'Pass it to me.'

Omar passes to him.

Daniel runs with ball and kicks it into gate.

Tu runs around after them, following them.

Eser watching from playhouse door, comes over towards gate.

Boys ignore her.

Eser goes to climbing frame.

Tu holding ball.

Daniel: 'Tu! Here!'

Tu gives ball to Daniel, looking pleased about it.

Daniel kicks it in gate.

Daniel (triumphant):'I scored it!'

Here, Eser watches the boys, but they do not allow her to play with the football. She often plays basketball and kicks a football around, but never gets to play in the games. Tu tries to join in, but he does not display sufficient knowledge of football so he fails in his attempts to join the game. However, he is allowed to join as a peripheral participant, trying to copy the actions and handling the ball. When there were more balls in play, football games seemed to be much more mixed ability and easier for younger boys to join, whereas when only one ball was available, the more experienced, more skilled boys took over the action. Girls were usually excluded, no matter how many balls were in play.

In the following episode in the Reception playground there are two balls available. Ayla is the only girl to have any access to them during the whole lunch play. The episode is typical in that only the boys play the football games, but remarkable because Ayla tries to have a go.

Ayla to BM: 'I want to play with the football.'

BM: 'Well, they are playing football over there, can you go and join in?'

Ayla goes over to where six boys playing a vigorous game with red football – Ayla gets hold of the ball and throws it into the game.

Boys don't pass to her.

She gives up after two minutes, goes over and complains to dinner supervisor, who tells her to play with the hoops. She goes and stacks up the hoops.

When I asked boys about their favourite games, they frequently said it was football. They described details of the games and became animated and definite about the fact that football is a game for boys, not girls. In a typical conversation, Ben, then in his first term in Reception, explains to me why girls do not play football:

> Ben: 'I'm a boy. I play football. Girls can't play football.'
>
> BM: 'I know lots of girls who play football. Leonie and Jala in your class, they like to play football.'
>
> Ben: 'No, girls can't play football 'cos there's lots of boys. There's no room for girls.'
>
> BM: 'Do you think that's fair?'
>
> Ben: 'Girls just don't want to play. All the boys let *me* play.'

I think Ben is being honest in this discussion and pinpoints a dilemma of gender dualism. He undoubtedly wants to be correctly positioned as a boy who plays football, but can see that it is not fair if girls who want to play football cannot join in. So he comes up with the explanation that girls don't play football because they do not want to. When he says that there are lots of boys playing football so 'there's no room for girls', he sums up what I painstakingly documented over eighteen months. It was not so much that there was not enough space in the playground for girls to join in, although the area for ball games in the Reception playground was quite small. What happened was that some boys dominated all the action and however much space there was, boys expanded their activities to fill it. Football was a marker of *hegemonic masculinity* in the school.

Apprentice participation in play technologies

My analysis of the following episodes in the Nursery garden highlights some of the conflicts and negotiations involved in apprentice participation in play technologies. It is Tu's third term, but he is still trying to join the big boys' group. In the following episode, Tu is eager to be accepted as one of the big boys but his football skills and knowledge of English are quite limited. He tries to gain acceptance by an overture of providing additional balls for the game. Ryan rejects this. Ryan and Lewis are established full-timers, who often play a serious game of football using the entrance gate as a goal. They use football terms and display skills and knowledge of the game. They wear football shirts and talk about football teams.

Nursery Garden

Ryan and Lewis with big ball, kicking goals against the gate.

Tu takes two balls to Ryan. No reaction from Ryan.

Tu gets another ball and tries to kick it in goal.

Jake accidentally (?) kicks his ball so that the ball hits Tu on the nose.

...

Later, on the carpet at Story time.

Daniel to Mrs Jones: 'Tu had blood on his nose.'

Mrs Jones: 'Why, what happened?'

Daniel: "Cos Jake kicked the ball on his nose.'

Mrs Jones: 'Oh, so it was a real footballer's injury. That happens to footballers sometimes. My grownup sons play football and they sometimes have injuries like that.'

Tu still looks subdued. (I think he was quite hurt, and I am not convinced it was an accident).

In this episode, Tu tries to join in the big boys' game, and gets injured. When Daniel reports this later at carpet time, the teacher refers to it as 'real footballer's injury', thus promoting Tu's status as a football boy, and football as an approved game for adult men, fraught as it is with dangers of injury.

Tu is also learning that it is acceptable for boys to dominate girls. In the following episode, which took place a fortnight after the football injury, Tu tries to dominate Fifi, a girl then in her first term at Nursery. She successfully resists Tu's bid for power.

Fifi is pushing a buggy with a doll in it round the area outside the play house.

Tu goes to Fifi, teasing her, grabs hold of dolls' buggy, advancing on her.

Fifi: 'No!' (Tu goes on pushing the buggy in front of Fifi. She goes over and tells Mrs Chen, who says 'Tu just want to look, let him look.' (Mrs Chen did not see what he was doing, but I saw he was deliberately disrupting her game with the buggy.)

Fifi goes back to Tu, and she advances on him, stands over him holding the buggy.

Fifi: 'Hey, that my buggy!'

Tu runs off, grabbing hold of another empty buggy and pushing it across the play area.

Fifi shouts after him: 'Hey, you need to have baby in the buggy!'

Tu tries to exert power over Fifi, using physical force. Despite Mrs Chen's failure to take her complaint seriously, Fifi succeeds in stopping Tu from spoiling her game. She tells him the buggy is hers, and demonstrates that unlike him, she knows that you need to have a baby in the buggy in order to play with it properly.

This is also the first term in Nursery for two boys, Damien and Ervin. In the episodes below, the boys try to join in the football games with the older boys. Fifi is also keen to play with the football, but faces considerable opposition from Tu and Damien.

> Daniel and Jake come out, kicking a football, big gestures, taking up lots of space by the gate. Damien runs over and tries to join in but they do not pass the ball to him.
>
> Tu tries to join in, kicking another green ball.
>
> Fifi gets another ball, but Damien kicks it away from her.
>
> Fifi: 'You bad boy!'
>
> Fifi goes to get another ball. Tu comes over and tries to take that one.
>
> Fifi: 'No Tu!' (She takes the ball, runs with it across the play space and climbs with it to top of climbing frame.)
>
> Tu does not follow her.

Damien persists in trying to join the football game, but, as yet, is not accepted. He is learning that it is acceptable to take a ball from a girl. Fifi succeeds in getting control of a ball, but only by removing herself from the football game. In the following weeks, I observed her playing with the older girls, Tagan and Oni, with increasing frequency, watching them and begin-ning to join in their play with buggies and dolls. As a girl, she is not accepted as a peripheral participant in the boys' ball games. In contrast, Damien and Ervin are beginning to learn the rules for participation. Below Ervin is finding out that football is the game that carries status.

> Damien and Ervin are trying to throw balls into the basketball net. Damien keeps missing but Ervin is getting the ball in frequently.
>
> Damien goes to get a bike and rides it round and round near the basketball net, watching Ervin.
>
> Ervin climbs to top of climbing frame and is trying to throw a ball into net from top of climbing frame, tries to get other boys to join in.

> Ervin calls to Daniel: 'Come and play netball!'
>
> Daniel: 'No, *we* are playing football' (goes over to the gate with Jake and Ryan).

Ervin's ball skills are good, but he has not yet learned that football is the game that conveys status. He invites Daniel to play netball with him but Daniel rebuffs him. Daniel is an older full-time boy who is particularly skilled at football. Daniel takes the lead in organising the boys' football games, and he makes it clear to Ervin that Ervin is not part of this football group.

Older boys often took on the role of instructor. In the next episode, Omar, an established older full-timer who often chose to play football, is keen to show newcomers Ervin and Fifi how to play bat and ball. This play episode shows in detail how children negotiate relationships and learn about and explore gender roles through play.

> Ervin gets two bats and a small ball, gives one to Damien.
>
> Damien goes over towards gate, watching older boys playing football.
>
> Fifi gets another bat.
>
> Omar comes over, picks up bat, to Ervin 'Can I show you how to do it? I'll show you how you play.' (demonstrates, hits ball across into grass)
>
> Omar:'Yeah, that's how to do it!' (pleased with himself, smiling)
>
> Fifi: 'I didn't bat it! You didn't bat it to me!'
>
> Ervin to Mrs Chen: 'He batted it!' (complaining, indicating Omar hit it onto the grass. Then Ervin hits another ball away from Omar)
>
> Omar to Fifi: 'You play with me too!'
>
> Fifi: 'No! I'm not playing with you, you didn't bat it to me!'
>
> Omar: 'I'm Batman. You super girl.
>
> Fifi smiles and bats ball to him.
>
> Omar bats back to her.
>
> Ervin bats to Omar. (All three play together for several minutes).

Omar begins by trying to teach Ervin, but when Ervin ceases to be compliant, Omar turns his attention to Fifi. She asserts herself by saying that as he has not been batting to her she does not want to play with him. Omar tries to gain Fifi as a playmate by introducing a superhero theme. He declares himself to be Batman (an important and powerful role, as well as a play on the word 'bat',) and says she can be 'supergirl', a fairly important role. Fifi accepts his overture, and there follows a cooperative sequence where the three children play bat and ball, taking it in turns to bat. A period of dispute often preceded a period of cooperative play like this, when girls and boys managed to negotiate episodes of play with each other.

In the following play episode Damien, then in his first term in Nursery, gets opportunities to develop ball skills as an apprentice participant at the basketball net. The older girls, Tagan and Jala encourage him, but are themselves pushed out by Jake. I documented many episodes similar to this, when boys took over equipment and space from girls, and girls either put up with this or protested only mildly.

> Older boys playing football. Damien tried to join but was refused.
>
> Damien holding a ball on own and running round basketball net on his own. Damien: 'I'm the leader!'
>
> Jala with ball at basketball, throwing and getting ball into net consistently.
>
> Jala: 'Yeah!'(jumping up and down triumphantly).
>
> Jake joins her at the net and pushes in front of her with another ball. He throws and misses, runs to gate end of playground to play football.

Damien and Ervin and Tu gradually became legitimate peripheral participants in the community of practice of boys in the Nursery playground. They learned about football through observing the older boys, and took part in aspects of the game, such as kicking and throwing balls, and developing hand and eye coordination through playing with bats and balls and basketball. Fifi, a girl who enjoyed ball games, had to struggle to get a share of the ball. Fifi's experience is typical of my findings, showing how girls in the Nursery playground were frequently prevented by boys from taking control of the ball, and how boys often excluded girls if they tried to join in football games. Fifi was unusual in her persistence, but even she became discouraged and went increasingly to play with the buggies with other girls.

Basketball

I often saw boys and girls playing together at the basketball net in the Nursery playground. Play at the basketball net was less formal, more inclusive, more experimental. It had fewer rules and emotional investments than use of footballs or skipping ropes but was not played without power struggles and conflicts, and older boys often dominated the action. In the Nursery playground, the basketball net provided a focus for individual children to throw a ball, and sometimes to throw to each other as well.

Basketball play shows us how children became legitimate peripheral participants in girls' and boys' playground communities of practice. Peripheral participation requires that the apprentice learner be engaged in an activity that is connected to the main activity. Lave and Wenger (1991) give the example of butchers' apprentices in supermarkets, who are given tasks away from the main activity of butchering, so that their participation is legitimate, but removed rather than peripheral. In a similar way, playing basketball was legitimate peripheral participation in ball games, but it was removed from football so does not amount to peripheral participation in football. Basketball games gave the players the chance to develop ball skills, but boys did not generally accept that girls have the skills and knowledge to play football. Having good ball skills did not enable girls to be accepted into football games. And amongst the older boys it was football prowess that carried status in both the Nursery and Reception.

Research conclusions

How does it happen that skipping ropes are understood by children to be for girls and footballs for boys? Ash Vale early years staff encouraged all boys and girls to play with ropes and balls in the Nursery garden, and no adults told children that skipping is for girls and football for boys. However, as new children worked out the rules for belonging to the communities of practice of femininities and masculinities in the Nursery, they began to learn to use footballs and ropes in gendered ways.

Boys did not allow girls to join in football because they did not want their masculine preserve to be tainted by femininity. The rituals of football are so appealing to young boys because they are training to be apprentice men. This is demonstrated in their references to adult male footballers. Staff sometimes encouraged these aspirations. When they excluded girls and younger and less skilled boys, the older boys asserted their membership of a community of practice of hegemonic masculinity of boys, and laid claim to future membership of a community of adult men (Nespor, 1997; Paechter, 2007).

My research suggests that girls held on to skipping as a girls-only activity in situations where this was the only space they could claim for themselves. Boys dominated all other outdoor play spaces. Nadia says she does not play skipping with Charlie because he cannot skip. This might be true at a physical level; at this stage of Charlie's physical development he is less skilled at skipping than Nadia. But it is also true at an emotional level. He cannot skip because to do so would go against the norms of behaviour within the boys' community of practice in Reception, and he would risk rejection and ridicule from both boys and girls. Girls derived pleasure from their knowledge about skipping, and the activity was encouraged and supported by female staff. However, unlike football, skipping is not something that adults do, nor is it a highly paid, high status sport, to which girls can aspire.

Skipping provided girls with an inclusive group activity that was fun, relatively safe from injuries, approved of by adults, and understood to be for girls. It was not necessary to be particularly skilled to join a skipping game, and it was acceptable to make mistakes, although girls enjoyed showing that they knew the rhymes and could skip many times in the rope. Older girls initiated younger ones into the specific practices of jumping over the rope, rope turning and chanting rhymes.

Playing skipping games involved girls in enacting heteronormative scripts. Some rhymes, like 'Apple Pie', where the girls name a boy as their 'sweetie pie', enacted discourses of romantic love and heterosexuality (Epstein, 1997, 1999). As Epstein argues, rhymes like these are an activity through which heterosexuality is normalised, even if the girls do not think about it consciously.

My research in Ash Vale shows that children learned complex social rules while they developed skills for using play objects. Ropes and footballs carried symbolic and emotional significance within the girls' and boys' communities of practice. Children learned about the technologies as legitimate peripheral members of communities of practice of girls and boys, through observing older members and taking part in certain minor aspects of the games. Then gradually, they took a fuller part, and some went on to dominate and initiate changes in the games.

One of the most potent aspects of the pleasure the children derived arose from the same-sex dimension of the technologies. In other words, it is *because* skipping is understood to be for girls and football for boys that children wanted to participate and excel in these activities. Boys and girls policed the boundaries so strictly because to allow children of the opposite sex to use each other's technologies and gain appropriate knowledge would undermine and allow challenges to the individual and collective gendered power that goes with the use of ropes and footballs.

Reinforcing gender dualism

The Reception playground at lunch times was a key site for the transmission of gendered knowledge and the development of gendered identities. My data analysis shows that boys and girls played mostly in separate same-sex groups.

At lunchtimes Year 6 children were encouraged to volunteer to help lunch-time supervisors in the Reception playground. During my research period, all who volunteered were girls, except two boys who volunteered for a few sessions at the start of a new term. The girls were mostly very conscientious helpers. The lunchtime supervisor explained to me why she thought girls volunteered.

> Ms Lucas: 'The girls like to play with the little ones, and they do a good job of looking after them. And tidying up too. The boys don't want to be bothered, they want the time for their football. And if the boys do come over they just muck about.'

Ms Lucas draws on the discourse of oppositional gender when she thinks it is natural that girls would want to help with younger children, and that boys would want to play football, or that if boys do volunteer as helpers, they would not be helpful. The younger children saw only older girls, not boys, helping at playtime, and this reinforced the discourse of gender dualism. The Year 6 girls helped the lunchtime supervisors to clear up at the end of dinner play, and some of the younger girls did small jobs such as collecting up hoops. Many of the boys carried on playing chasing games and often started play-fighting games whilst the clearing up was being done. Meals supervisors would often shout to these boys, 'Stop being silly, boys', and often called them several times to line up when the bell went, 'Boys, boys, hurry up!' In this way, some younger girls became legitimate peripheral participants in the com-munity of practice of 'sensible helpful' girls, in contrast to boys' 'silly selfish-ness' (Francis, 1998).

A Year 6 girl, Carlie, set up dancing sessions at lunchtimes for the younger children. She organised this very efficiently, with taped music and she and a couple of other Year 6 girls demonstrated the routines. My observations show that it was predominantly girls who joined in these dancing sessions, although a few boys imitated the moves, rather self-consciously, keeping close together on the edge of the group, and with much laughter. Carlie was keen to include boys as well as girls, but realised that this was a hard task be-cause dance was seen in the school as mostly a feminine activity.

> Carlie to BM: 'I'm helping them with their steps and that. Its all girls at the moment, but we're gonna change it and get some boys involved. It's a bit girlie now' (swivels her hips). I go to Dance Club after school. It's mostly girls there too.'

As Francis (2000) notes, discourses of gender dualism are often self-perpetuating, as oppositional gender performances become a key cornerstone of children's identities.

Implications for early years education

My analysis of children's play practices shows how children learned to perform oppositional practices of masculinity or femininity through the use of skipping ropes and footballs. Young children observed the play practices of older children, and observed the expectations held by adults about their gendered behaviours, and acted accordingly. Many children derived emotional as well as physical pleasure from playing with ropes and footballs.

Young children in early years settings often spend long periods of time each day in free play activities in the playground. What play resources are provided can affect how children relate together. For example, I observed that younger, less skilled boys and girls enjoyed play with balls when there were plenty supplied, but these children were excluded by dominant boys when only a few balls were available.

Early years educators need to ensure that all children have access to play equipment. The lunch time play is a key site for the production of gendered identities and can amount to a sixth of the time spent by children in school each day. Children are pressured to conform to oppositional gender norms and early years educators need to focus on how and what children are learning during this play time.

Checklist for action for gender equity

- Monitor the use of play equipment in free play times and lunch breaks. Observe who uses play objects eg skipping ropes and footballs. How are play spaces used? Do some children dominate? Are some children excluded? Talk to colleagues, dinner supervisors and children about play patterns. Talk to children about their play choices.

- Remember that children have emotional investments in playing with gendered play objects such as ropes and footballs. Many feel they need to belong to same-sex social groups at playtime. For some children play time can be long and scary. Use your understanding to provide safe spaces and help children explore pleasurable possibilities for play.

- Provide plenty of play equipment so that younger, less dominant children can have access to skipping ropes, footballs and so on. If football is dominating the play space, redesign the space so that other activities are possible eg provide an area for music using junk materials, mark out number squares, and develop garden plots.

■ Support children who want to cross gender boundaries in outdoor play eg provide girls-only football times.

■ Encourage older children to help with activities in Nursery and Reception playgrounds, and provide opportunities for non-gender-stereotyped activities such as boys taking part in skipping and girls playing football.

■ Do not reinforce gender dualism at play times by encouraging girls to help with clearing up and allowing boys to opt out. Avoid calling out 'Boys stop...' or 'You girls...' Try instead to use children's names when praising or reprimanding them.

4

Masculine and feminine
play activities

This chapter explores how children learned to *embody* aspects of masculinity or femininity in early years classes and how schooling practices reinforced gender dualism. In Chapters 2 and 3 we saw how children learned from each other that some play activities were for girls and some were for boys. We saw how boys dominated particular spaces in classrooms and playgrounds. This chapter discusses how children learned about symbols and markers of femininity and masculinity and how they struggled either to police or to cross gender borders in their play.

As Hatcher (1995) points out, it is important to study how children actively construct their own cultures but also to theorise the relationship between the worlds of children and adult cultures, by exploring the ways children's cultures are shaped by adult discourses. Communities of practice, again, provide a framework for the theory. Girls and boys learn about gender by participating as peripheral and, later, full members of children's communities of practice. They also participate as legitimate peripheral members in adult communities of practice (Paechter, 2007). For example, boys talked about wearing clothes that linked them to wider communities of masculinity. Football team shirts were particularly prized, and staff often commented on these with approval.

Carpet

Mrs Clarke: 'Damien, come up and show us all your Man U Tshirt. My son supports that team.'

Some boys used superhero shirts to demonstrate that they were correctly positioned within communities of masculinity.

Mani: 'I got a spiderman shirt indoors.'

Markers of femininity

Girls had usually learned that pink is for girls before they came to school, from adults' comments and behaviour, from media images and advertising. They had been dressed in pink and given pink toys. When girls joined the Nursery class they learned to embody pink for girls from messages from older members of the communities of practice of nursery girls, first as apprentice participants and then full members. They learned that pink can be a symbol for powerful girl things. They also learned about pink for girls from young boys, who used pink for girls as a way of keeping girls out of certain activities and exerting power over them in specific play situations (see p108). Pink for girls was used in play practices as a marker of femininity by both the girls and the boys.

An important marker of belonging to the girls' community of practice involved having the correct appearance. This affected what activities the girls engaged in. It involved having pink clothes, elaborate hair styles, fashionable shoes and choosing appropriate dressing up outfits. There were variations in style; for example African girls often had braids and hair extensions. But wearing pink was a common marker of girlhood. Even though children at this age do not choose and buy their own clothes, they are very aware of the importance of having girls' clothes and accessories (Blaise, 2005). The norm of pink for girls was embodied by individual girls in their clothing, hair ornaments, jewellery, writing and drawing materials, toys, lunch boxes, school bags, coats, socks and fashion items. There was a sea of pink in the Nursery class when girls sat on the carpet. In Reception the children were required to wear school uniform, so differences in clothing were less marked when they moved up but hairstyles and shoes remained masculine and feminine markers.

Girls in Ash Vale Nursery showed a great concern about their appearance. Some made remarks to each other about their clothes, as overtures of friendship.

> Sara to Hong: 'I like your skirt. I like your pink shoes.' Hong smiles. The two girls sit close, lots of eye contact.

Some girls expressed great interest, preferences and concern about clothes, hairstyles and shoes. In conversation with a female member of the Nursery staff, Yomi draws on her home experience.

> Yomi to Mrs Jones: 'I like doing fashion.'
>
> Mrs Jones: 'Does your sister like fashion?'

Left: Molly: 'I got a bag and silver shoes for wedding.'

Yomi: 'My sister like fashion. She likes to do, she likes to, shows off, she wears Nigeria clothes. My sister wear high heels.'

Mrs Jones: 'That's nice.'

Yomi: 'She got red hair and black hair.'

Mrs Jones: 'Yes. Your sister has textured hair. She uses dye.'

As they got older, the girls developed their knowledge and aware- ness of makeup, clothes and feminine fashion. Blaise (2005) docu- ments ways in which girls in a preschool in USA embody and enact heteronormative practices of femininity, displaying knowledge of female fashion, makeup and beauty and positioning themselves within discourses of *emphasised femininity*, enacting narratives where they dress up and make themselves beautiful for princes and imaginary boyfriends. Most girls in Ash Vale early years classes drew frequently on discourses of female fashion. Ayo, in her first term in Reception, drew a picture of her herself and her sister wearing makeup and high heeled boots.

Ayo: 'I like to wear my sister's clothes. And she has high boots. She has pink lipstick. It's for bigger girls, my sister says. My Mum has red lipstick.'

Her classmate, Molly draws a picture of herself in a long pink dress and high heels.

Molly: 'I am going to my sister's party. My new dress. And shoes'.

In their imaginary portrayal of themselves, Ayo and Molly position them- selves as legitimate peripheral members of teenage and adult communities of practice of femininity. Below, Zuhre tells me about what she likes to do in the playground. Although she said she likes playing football and jumping on the blocks, her picture of herself shows her in a long dress with high heeled shoes.

Zuhre (to BM): 'My shoes have heels with spikes, go tap tap tap on the floor.'

Many of the girls drew elaborate pictures of themselves in princess costumes, party and wedding dresses and often portrayed their faces with bright big lip- stick, exaggerated eyelashes and big hairdos. These pictures were in marked contrast to boys' self portraits, which usually showed them in action: playing ball, eating, running or jumping. Ravi's drawing of himself playing football is typical. He has coloured his face in black to show his skin colour.

Right: Ravi's self portrait

The next episode illustrates Nina and Madia's preoccupation with their appearance.

Nursery Carpet Storytime

Mrs Jones (in front of everybody, reprovingly): 'Nina, pull your skirt down!' (Nina looks embarrassed and tugs her skirt down. There is a fashion for girls to wear very short tight skirts over leggings or tights at the moment. The skirts tend to ride up).

...

TV time

Nina to Madia (in concerned voice, gesturing to her legs): 'Look, dere!'

Leans across and touches Madia's trousers, pointing out a muddy mark on her white trousers.

Madia: 'Oh my goodness!' (Looks in consternation at the muddy stains, then at Nina, eyes wide in horror, then starts to scrub ineffectually at her trousers).

Possibly, Nina noticed and commented on Madia's problem with her clothes because Mrs Jones had just commented on Nina's. Mrs Jones is policing Nina, and Nina is policing Madia, to make sure girls are neat, clean and modest. Furthermore, 'My goodness', or more often, 'goodness me', was used by teachers to convey disapproval. Here Madia is using the same phrase to criticise herself for having got her white clothes dirty playing in the garden. Nina and Madia are learning that it is their responsibility as girls to adapt their behaviour to accommodate their clothing and to pay close attention to their appearance and monitor how they look to others (Foucault, 1977). This is how girls learned to monitor their own behaviour and conform to specific aspects of femininity.

Paechter (2007) discusses Foucault's (1977) development of the concept of *panoptic surveillance* from Bentham's design of a model prison, the Panopticon. Bentham's prison was designed to instil good behaviour in prisoners by placing guards in a central darkened watch tower, and prisoners in lighted cells so they knew they could be being watched at any time. The idea was that prisoners would learn to internalise good behaviour and police themselves, so there would be no need for heavy surveillance. Foucault develops this concept of surveillance, showing how panoptic mechanisms of surveillance permeate social relations through a 'disciplinary modality of power' (Foucault, 1977:216). One group of people exert a disciplinary gaze upon another to induce conformity and regulate behaviours.

Paechter (2007) applies the concept of *panoptic surveillance* to communities of practice of masculinities and femininities: members exert a disciplinary gaze on one another, and this encourages conformity to the gender norms of the group. She suggests that panoptic surveillance is particularly important in early childhood communities of practice of masculinity and femininity, as it affects the way in which newcomers learn to engage in practices as legitimate peripheral participants. Here Nina and Madia were learning to police each other's appearance as girls.

Markers of masculinity

Boys in Ash Vale early years classes learned to take an active part in three key hegemonic practices of masculinity in the setting: superhero play based on battles, football, and construction (including Lego, train and car play). I use the term battle play to describe the fighting games, because this is what the boys called it, and it emphasises the serious strategic work that took place in these games. Staff used the term 'playfighting', which has rather different connotations.

The concept of *hegemonic masculinity*, developed by Connell (1987, 2002), who drew on Gramsci's analysis of class relations in Italy, underpins my analysis of children's gendered play. Hegemony refers to a social ascendancy of certain groups that is achieved not through brute force or violence but through cultural processes and institutions. Hegemony is maintained and reproduced by structuring discourse so that unequal power relations within the *status quo* are understood as natural, inevitable and taken for granted. Hegemonic masculinity positions some men, and all women, as subordinate inferior *Others*.

> The forms of femininity and masculinity constituted at this level are stylised and impoverished. Their interrelation is centred on a single structural fact, the global dominance of men over women. (Connell, 1987:183)

Hegemonic forms of masculinity take different forms in different cultural contexts. 'Masculine' and 'feminine' are often used as though their meanings are fixed and permanent, but the meanings change depending on historical, political and social and attitudes (Buchbinder, 1994). The concept of hegemonic masculinity helps explain how gendered power relations operate. But we must examine hegemonic masculinities in specific communities of practice to avoid essentialising and stereotyping masculine behaviour (Paechter, 2007). We learn to position ourselves as correctly gendered in social situations through masculine or feminine behaviour. This affects how we feel about ourselves as boys and girls, men and women. Certain taken-for-granted positions reinforce and confirm what boys think they already know about masculinity, such as it is manly to be physically strong, that real men are heterosexual, or that men naturally tend to be good at football.

Paechter (2007) argues that it is vitally important for gender differences to be seen as 'natural', and taken-for-granted, so that local hegemonic masculine power relations can be preserved and reproduced. Boys learn that legitimate participation in communities of masculinity confers considerable benefits, and they seek to reproduce local hegemonic practices of masculinity, for example through display of skills and knowledge about sport (Skelton, 2001; Swain, 2003). This can be seen clearly in how boys in Ash Vale learned to value hegemonic masculine play.

Taking part in battles and associated superhero play was a central marker of masculinity in early years classes. The objects of knowledge and physical attributes many boys valued were related to these activities, and boys often had to work hard to be accepted as full participants. Part of the way they could claim membership of boys' communities of practice was through demonstrating their physical skills, ball skills in football, construction skills, skills in running, jumping, and their physical strength and endurance in battle play. They could also gain acceptance by demonstrating appropriate knowledge, of the game of football, and of storylines as superheroes. The relative positions of boys within the pecking order in Ash Vale were determined by other boys, regulated through football, construction and battle play. Boys who were new to Nursery and Reception learned the rules for dominant masculinity through observation and imitation rather than direct instruction. Boys learned to exclude girls from football, construction and battle play. Some girls confirmed the right of boys to participate in these practices of hegemonic masculinity by deferring to boys, although some resisted being positioned outside them.

The rules for dominant masculinity are mostly learned through observation and imitation rather than direct instruction. Buchbinder (1994) calls the competition between males the 'Masculinity Stakes'. In patriarchal societies only men can confer masculinity, although women can confirm it. Dominant men determine the relative positions of other men within the pecking order. This has important consequences for young boys because they must work out how to behave in order to belong to a male community of practice, and they must compete if they want to achieve a dominant position. To compete, they need to figure out what objects of knowledge and physical attributes are valued within the group, and find ways of exercising power over others to achieve status. Some boys reject or refuse to take part in the 'Masculinity Stakes' by embodying alternative masculinities, but this carries the risk of exclusion and public humiliation from peers and older males. Groups of dominant men and boys position those who do not conform as not only subordinate, but not properly masculine at all (Connell, 1995).

Boys in Ashvale conferred masculinity upon each other, and they had to compete if they wanted to achieve a dominant position. It is no coincidence that the two key masculine marked play practices of football and battles have highly competitive elements. Dominant boys who defined and dominated hegemonic masculinities did not allow younger or weaker boys to join their games.

In this football episode, Damien and Malik are both in their first term at Nursery. Damien comes and takes a ball to play with on his own and Malik tries to join a football game but Jake tells him to go away. However, Damien and Malik have watched the dominant boys, and store up the knowledge for the future.

> Daniel: 'Let's play football.'
>
> Ryan: 'Yeah!'
>
> Daniel: 'This is what you do, you do this.' (demonstrates kicking ball at gate to score a goal.)
>
> Three balls in play.
>
> Malik watching.
>
> Jake: 'This is my Chelsea ball.'
>
> Damien comes and takes a ball runs off with it by himself to other end of playground.
>
> Older boys kicking balls at gate. Daniel Jake, Ben, Omar
>
> Daniel takes ball from Jake, kicks it.
>
> Malik comes over, by gate.
>
> Jake (to Malik): 'Hey, *no!*'
>
> Malik goes to sand pit.

The boys in Ash Vale learned to value certain masculine performances, and fashion their bodies in specific ways so as to position themselves as strong in relation to other boys, and superior to girls. Browne (2004) notes how young boys embody physical gestures to explore aspects of hegemonic masculinity, by positioning themselves as dominant, strong, brave and physically agile. Similarly, the boys in my research setting used their football and battle games to embody and explore these aspects of hegemonic masculinity, drawing on discourses that circulate beyond the school, in media images and home communities.

Another key marker of masculinity for the boys was avoidance of anything feminine. New boys in Nursery learned from oldtimers that pink is for girls and that they should avoid anything coloured pink as if it were a pollutant.

> Kumi (disgusted voice): 'That a girl pen. Don't use that!' (It is pink)

How boys scorn girls and stigmatise boys who perform anything connected to femininity, by Othering girlishness and distancing themselves from it has been widely documented (eg Browne, 2004). Renold (2005) explores how boys attempt to resist hegemonic masculine practices by drawing on misogynistic discourses. It is hugely important for boys to distance themselves from practices of femininity.

> Because masculine-marked forms of knowledge convey and confer actual power on those who 'master' them, it becomes important for boys (both for themselves and to help sustain hegemonic social forms) to claim privileged access to this knowledge, and hence this power, and to deny them to their female peers. (Paechter, 2003:71)

Borderwork

Children explored gender in their play through borderwork – instances where children police gender boundaries to keep girls and boys separate, instances where children cross gender boundaries and episodes when girls and boys explore activities and relationships with each other. Borderwork (Thorne, 1993) often involves the maintenance of distinctions between girls and boys, in dress, behaviours, use of space and body. The very phrase 'opposite sex' emphasises the differences between boys and girls, and evokes a gender dualism.

Borderwork is enormously important because it is through this that children explore and try out different behaviour. Children often try to understand what the gender boundaries are, and to strengthen them. Sometimes they test and push the gender boundaries; sometimes they struggle to break through them. I use 'border' as a spatial metaphor, and it has connotations of power struggles and conflict. Borders are created to separate out areas. Geographical and political borders are sometimes established along physical features of the land, such as rivers and mountains. In school gender border-work is often spatial, as children claim and negotiate access to areas of class-rooms and playgrounds and borders are often negotiated at entrances and doorways.

Relational aspects of borderwork

My research focused on gender borders, but it is important to take account of ways in which gender borderwork relates to other borderwork. Gender borders often relate to home/school borders and borderwork around race, ethnicity and cultural differences. Children in Ash Vale were very aware of ethnic differences and struggled to understand their salience. There were six-teen ethnic groups and thirteen languages were spoken in addition to English in the Nursery during the period I was doing my research. Ash Vale imple-mented equal opportunity policies and celebrated home languages and cul-tures in school assemblies and festivals.

However, staff did not encourage children to speak or write in their home languages in class or the playground. Bilingual support assistants were used in class as general assistants rather than as support for bilingual pupils. In Nursery, children were encouraged to take dual language books home, but the home book box was covered as soon as the children had chosen their books. This was a symbolic border between home and school cultures whereby chil-dren were expected to leave home languages at the classroom door. Speaking and writing English was given status, and the ability to speak or write another language was generally not valued or seen as relevant to learning.

Pearce (2005) shows how institutional 'colourblindness' and silence about issues of race and power make difficulties in school for children who are often struggling to understand ethnic differences. I found this in my research. Some children shared their pride in their home language and culture with me, in quiet moments, but the norm was for children not to refer to home cultures. The desirable knowledge within the classroom was school knowledge, the display of what it is to be a successful school pupil. There were usually no fixed rules, so the children had to interpret and generate meanings from the messages available to them, drawing on their experiences of home com-munities, and those they encountered in the Nursery and Reception classes.

The children I worked with often made comments that showed they were thinking about issues of skin colour and difference.

Reading 'Marcellus'

Omar: 'He be friends with that boy (Points to the black boy). But he not be friends with him (points to white boy.)

BM: 'Why do you think he won't be friends with him?'

Omar: 'Because he not black.'

...

Drawing pictures

Jala: 'My Mummy is light. My Daddy is brown. Like me.'

Researchers including Shain (2003) and George (2007) emphasise the importance of exploring differences within as well as between ethnicities. George (2007) found that girls positioned themselves, and were positioned in a variety of ways within discourses of race, ethnicity and schooling. George's research explores the complexities in how a group of preadolescent girls negotiate friendship across ethnic divisions. Some, but not all, prioritised friendships with girls from similar cultural backgrounds. 'It is unsurprising that black girls, with their different history and heritage rooted in past racism, as well as different futures dictated by institutional racism, will make friends with girls who share similar backgrounds' (George, 2007).

I occasionally heard children use skin colour and cultural differences to insult each other.

Hong to Mrs Teal: 'He (Kumi) say I speak China girl' (aggrieved tone, looking indignant and insulted)

Kumi looking inscrutable, standing close by (waiting to be told off, defend himself?)

Mrs Teal (to Hong and Kumi): 'You can speak Chinese, Kumi can speak Yoruba. You are such clever children.'

Hong looks fed up.

Although Mrs Teal's response is positive because it values the languages they both speak, it has not satisfied Hong because it does not deal with Kumi's perceived intention to insult her. Is he insulting her as a girl, or as a person who speaks Chinese, or both? Usually when children reported insults, staff took them seriously. However insulting remarks like 'China girl' need to be understood in the wider context of power relations within the Nursery and beyond, where competence in languages other than English was undervalued. English was the language of instruction and demonstrated that you were a proper school child. Even when children shared the same home language, they did not speak to each other in it. Nobody told them not to, but they picked up on cues that it was not something you did in school (Pearce, 2005). Madia and Nina were close friends but I never heard them speak in Spanish together, except occasionally when a Spanish speaking bilingual support assistant was working with them. Jason was a Twi speaker, and was a confident established Reception boy, but he was not encouraged to speak Twi with a new girl, Paige, even when she was struggling to understand class routines.

In the following episode, Yomi and Ayo emphasise their shared pride in their identity as Black African English speaking girls, and in doing so, they exclude a new girl, Madia. Yomi accuses Madia of 'talking Chinese' although Madia's home language is actually Spanish.

Yomi, Ayo and Madia at collage table.

Yomi: 'You talk Chinese. You're not English' (to Madia, hostile voice)

Ayo: 'We talk normal than you' (boasting, staring at Madia)

Yomi: 'We talk African' (proudly)

Harrison (overhearing, calls pleasantly, matter of fact voice): 'She has a Chinese mouth.'

Madia gets up from table, goes to fetch apron, fills containers in water tray. (Ignoring comments, removing herself, says nothing, stiff body and frozen face)

...

Yomi (loud, challenging): 'I told her she talks Chinese, (pause) and you are a nut' (playfully to Ayo in contrast to hostile voice she used to Madia)

Ayo: (jokey) 'No I'm not!'

Yomi: 'Yes you are!' (Repeated several times like a chant, smiling and laughing).

Madia was new in Nursery that term. She appears upset by the incident and removes herself from the collage table to the water tray. This is still within earshot of the collage table, so she hears Ayo and Yomi's subsequent remarks. Their playful exchange emphasises that she does not belong in their friendship group. English is the language of instruction and also social interaction. Ayo and Yomi are performing competent pupil in this incident, both in their ability to use English, and in asserting their superiority as older girls. Whilst the staff would not condone their boastful position, the Nursery culture endorses their attitude, in the sense that children are expected to speak English in class. When Yomi says 'We talk African', she is identifying herself with Ayo, as Black girls who are proud of the way they talk. This adds a further dimension to their friendship, in that they can both take pride in 'talking African', although both are actually speaking to each other in English. Ayo's home language is Ijaw, and Yomi's is Yoruba.

Issues of race and ethnicity are entwined with issues of gender in complex ways in the children's interactions. Young children in my study were very aware of issues of race and ethnicity. This supports research with young children (Brown, 1998; Connolly, 1998; MacNaughton, 2000; Robinson and Jones Diaz, 2006) showing that children as young as 3 and 4 have awareness and understandings of issues of race, racism and ethnic differences, and draw on a range of discourses of race and gender in their interactions in preschool. Troyna and Hatcher's research (1992) into racism and children's cultures emphasises the importance of examining racism and the part played by 'race' within children's social relations. This stance is taken from Hall (1980) and Miles (1989) who emphasise the need to analyse how racism operates within specific historical situations and social processes.

Gender borders

In both Nursery and Reception the boys and girls learned to take part in masculine and feminine activities in separate spaces. A gender border was crossed when a child engaged in behaviour or used something more usually associated with the opposite sex. In the following fieldnote, Lan is distressed until she is offered a pink sticker, because she knows pink is the one for girls, and Paige learns that she should have asked for a pink one when the other girls police her choice.

> When children have finished work I invite them to choose a sticker picture of a toy. All the girls pick a pink one. When Lan comes to choose, there are no pink ones left. She just sits and stares at the stickers.
>
> BM: 'Do you want to choose one, Lan?'
>
> Chloe: 'She wants a girl one.'
>
> BM: 'Is the one you want not there Lan?'
>
> Lan: 'No.'
>
> I get out a spare sheet with all the stickers on it. Lan immediately points to the pink doll's house.
>
> Lan: 'I want that one.'

When Paige picks, she takes a car sticker. I overhear other girls telling her she has a 'boy' sticker. About 5 minutes later she brings it back and holds it out to me, indicating that she wants a different one. I offer her a full sheet to choose from and she points to the pink dolls house. Paige has been told that she has the 'wrong' sticker, and peer pressure has sent her back to get a proper 'girl one'.

In the episode below I am reading *Titch and Daisy* with Ayo and Amena. Both demonstrate to me their knowledge that girls and not boys wear pink hairbands. Amena goes on to demonstrate that she knows girls play with Barbies and boys play with Power Rangers, positioning herself as a girl within a discourse of gender difference whereby pink is understood as a marker of femininity. Liam demonstrates to Amena and me that he has the correct toys for a boy.

Ayo: (pointing to picture in story book) 'That a girl.'

BM: 'How can you tell?'

Ayo: 'She got a pink hairband.'

BM: 'Couldn't a boy wear a pink hairband?'

Amena (as if, are you kidding?) 'No,oh! Girls wear pink hairbands. I got a pink hairband. No boys.'

Ayo: 'The boy, he has to get his hair cut, he has to get it flat. (points to girl) She can wear a pink hairband, not a boy.'

Amena (to BM): 'I tell you a secret. (whispers in my ear) I got a Barbie singer. It's pink one.'

Ayo(looks fed up at being left out): 'Tell me Amena!'

Amena whispers to Ayo.

Amena: 'Shall I tell Liam?'

BM: 'Yes, why not.'

Amena: 'Liam, I got a Barbie singer.'

Liam: 'I got a Power Ranger and a Power Ranger gun.'

Amena: 'My brother got a Power Ranger.'

BM: 'Would you like a Power Ranger, Amena?'

Amena: 'No, I got ones for girls. Pink. Liam got a Power Ranger the same like my brother.'

Children were often careful to position themselves correctly as a boy or girl by selecting an appropriately gendered toy. In the following episode, when children are discussing pictures of toys, Oni initially wants a Spiderman, but then changes to a doll when Richard polices her choice.

> Oni: 'I like the Spiderman.'
>
> Richard: 'That's for boys not for girls.'
>
> Oni looks worried.
>
> BM: 'Oni can choose the spiderman if she wants.'
>
> Richard: 'No, it's for boys!'
>
> BM: 'You can choose the spiderman if you want Oni.'
>
> Oni (looks distressed): 'No! I want that one! (points to a Barbie doll).

It was very difficult for the children to choose the toys that are stereotypically associated with the opposite sex. When they tried to cross gender borders, their behaviour was usually policed by other children.

> Omar (points to the Barbie doll): 'I want to get that! I gonna get that for mine' (very enthusiastic).
>
> Jake to Omar: 'Like for a girl?!!' (disbelieving, jeering)
>
> Omar (long pause, looks at Jake, looks at the Barbie doll, then sadly, frowning, low voice): 'No,oo.'

Borders were invoked if children crossed into the territory of the opposite sex. Rules about these territories were implicit and not always rigorously enforced. This means that in less public situations, children were sometimes able to contest and cross borders, particularly when they were not in a same-sex group. This links to spaces, because some spaces in Nursery and playground were fiercely guarded as boys' or girls' territory, whereas others did not carry such gendered connotations. However, non-gender marked spaces sometimes became the focus for borderwork to establish gendered territory (climbing frame, water tray) so the matter is quite complicated and each instance has to be closely analysed for significant factors. Instances of successful border crossing and cooperation between boys and girls are often fleeting and less dramatic than instances of border policing, so they are easily missed.

Reinforcing gender dualism – space and embodiment

Essentialist discourses continue to be used to justify differences in educational provision for girls and boys. Formal and informal spatial schooling practices often differentiate, for example in the expectation that boys will need to move around more, be noisier, take up more space. Gordon and Lahelma (1996) found that some teachers would reprimand girls for moving about even though they do it less than boys, because it is less expected from girls.

A contemporary example of separate gendered spatial provision is the reported introduction of new teaching methods in elementary school classrooms in the United States. Purves reports that special teaching methods are being introduced with the aim of allowing boys to be more physically active during lesson times. A separate carpet area is provided for girls to sit on and talk. 'They are segregating the sexes and dumping desks to allow boys to sprawl and move in a new approach to learning in the US' (Purves, 2005). Many practices in Ash Vale reflect similar beliefs about gender differences and encourage children to enact them.

Some of the school rules reinforced gender difference. For example, the Nursery rule that children were not allowed to climb when wearing jewellery often prevented girls climbing, as we see here.

Climbing frame

Ryan shows Mrs Jones his socks, pulling up his trouser legs.

Mrs Jones:'Very nice Ryan. They look like men's socks.'

Ryan (very pleased face, grinning): 'Yeah, they're football socks.'

...

Tagan goes to climb.

Mrs Jones: 'No Tagan, you can't climb today you are wearing jewellery. Tell Mummy.'

Tagan goes over to Mrs Jones, taking off her ring.

Mrs Jones: 'No, don't take it off Tagan, you have got to leave it on. You've got to tell Mummy.'

Tagan is forbidden from going on the climbing frame because she is wearing a ring. She tries to resolve the problem by taking it off, but is not allowed to. Ryan gains Mrs Jones' attention and approval with his request that she look at his socks. Mrs Jones compliments Ryan's appearance, telling him his socks are like mens' socks, which positions him within the adult community of practice of men who wear football socks. Teacher approval consolidates Ryan's position as a central member of a community of masculinity. In contrast, teacher disapproval emphasises problematic aspects of femininity practice for Tagan.

Mrs Jones says to Tagan that she must tell her mother not to let her wear jewellery, thus making her responsible for her mother's behaviour, but not allowing her to decide for herself to take off her ring. The rule of no jewellery applies in theory to all the children, but I never saw a boy wearing anything that forbade him to climb.

Staff reinforced gender stereotyped behaviour without meaning to. They encouraged and praised girls for being helpful and many girls took pleasure in demonstrating knowledge of classroom rules, and helping staff. Thus the staff reinforced ideas that girls are well behaved and helpful and boys are naughty.

In the following episode Ayo and Zuhre enact helpful school girl in the public arena of the Nursery carpet. Fruit was provided for the Nursery children at snack time.

> Mrs Jones (to Ayo and Zuhre): 'You two girls here, can you be very kind and go and ask Mrs Clarke for the fruit please? ... What sensible carrying Zuhre, good girl.'
>
> (Ayo and Zuhre look very proud of themselves, carry the bowls of fruit carefully, put them on the table, and come back to the carpet demonstrating very restrained and correct posture, sit down and cross their arms and legs and sit up with very straight backs, like ideal schoolgirls.)
>
> Mrs Jones (approvingly): 'Very sensible!'

The two girls' movements appear slightly exaggerated, but they look very serious. This is a serious and public event, as it takes place on the carpet in front of the whole class. Ayo and Zuhre are performing good girl and good pupil, and the two roles are identical here. Neither of them habitually sat so correctly on the carpet – in fact both were frequently told to sit properly – but here they show Mrs Jones and the (younger) children that they know and can demonstrate the rules. They take pleasure in being the centre of attention and being praised by Mrs Jones. Mrs Jones is explicitly asking them to demonstrate and perform good pupil, which is so often identical to good girl. The role involves being kind, sensible, helpful, sharing with other children, following the teacher's instructions, sitting up straight, keeping one's own body controlled in its movements, walking slowly and carefully, doing things independently, not interfering with other people's bodies. Mrs Jones conveys approval and praise for Zuhre and Ayo through her smiles and comments. In theory, the correct way for boys to perform good pupil was for them to do the same. I have instances of boys being told to control their bodies, for example to sit properly on the carpet, but my data analysis shows girls to have been more frequently reprimanded and more closely monitored.

Schools are sites of normalisation; specifically they are sites for the construction and production of normal children. This has important implications for how children are positioned within gender discourses. Children in school are encouraged to conform to norms of behaviour, their minds and bodies are regulated, disciplined and controlled, and they are subject to constant surveillance and assessment (Foucault, 1977; Nespor, 1997).

Spaces in schools are designated for different purposes, and decisions are made about the location and movement of bodies in specific areas of the school. Teachers are expected to control children's movement and teach them to sit still, be quiet, and listen attentively in class. The organisation of school buildings, classrooms and teaching arrangements make it possible for teachers to engage in surveillance of pupils, reinforced by panoptic surveillance (Foucault, 1977). In the assembly hall in Ash Vale, children were seated in rows facing the headteacher, with form teachers positioned at the end of the rows of children, so all the children were under surveillance.

Similarly, all children in Nursery and Reception were required to sit on a carpet facing the teacher for periods of instruction, all within the gaze of the teacher. As Connolly (1998) notes, this kind of spatial organisation enables teachers to rely on self-regulation, as pupils do not know when the teacher is looking specifically at them. The headteacher's gaze from the front of the hall, or teacher's gaze from the front of the carpet, the naming of individuals who are not paying attention and the occasional public humiliation of individuals who are misbehaving all demonstrate to all of the children that their behaviour is being monitored. Connolly (2004), I found that teachers' perceptions of discipline were often gendered. They expected girls to be passive and boys to be more disruptive.

Certain schooling practices sanction, reinforce and even create gender differences. Sometimes this is deliberate, as for example in the management of playgrounds in the US in the early 20th Century (Gagen, 2000). Gagen draws on Butler's work (1990) to show how playground organisers sought to instil heterosexist gender norms through spatial practices in the learning environments of the playground. Separate, segregated playground provision for boys and girls required children to pursue different activities and use their bodies in different ways. There were two types of playground, mixed to the age of 12, and a separate playground for older boys. Older girls remained with the younger children, as helpers, prefiguring their future roles as mothers and domestic servants. Children were directed towards differentiated bodily styles: the boys played team games, designed to encourage obedience to authority and physical endurance, whereas the girls performed patriotic songs and dances. This separate provision was justified on grounds that the children were being taught to express their natural gender identities.

> Rather than acknowledge the regulatory framework that was responsible for inducing masculine and feminine performances, instructors advance that children were merely expressing their new-found and true identity. (Gagen, 2000: 220)

It is the implied naturalness of dualistic gender frameworks that obscures the political aspects of inequitable gender constructions (Butler, 1990). Gagen's research has many parallels with my own, in that adults often explained children's gendered behaviours by appealing to 'natural differences'.

Children who resisted dominant practices of masculinity and femininity found their efforts curtailed or ridiculed. Some institutional practices of the school reinforced, normalised and encouraged gender dualism. The Christmas Christian Nativity play took up much time in the Autumn Term and was rigid in the allocation and performance of gender roles. Boys were kings and girls were angels. In the following episode, Omar tries to take the part of an angel in the Nursery Christmas play. The teacher and his classmates make it clear that he cannot.

Carpet time

Omar (grinning, puts hand up): 'I'm an angel.'

Mrs Jones (ignores Omar):'Madison, I like your hair clip, what a beautiful butterfly you have got in your hair. Do you want to do dancing?'

Madison shakes her head.

Omar: '*I* do.'

Mrs Jones (affectionately): 'No, because you are a *king* (makes this sound important) King Omar.'

....Fruit time

Mrs Jones: 'Some of you are going to do dancing.'

Omar: 'I am.'

Harrison (firmly): '*No*, you are not. (scathingly) Are you a girl?'

Omar (nodding): 'Yeah!'

Harrison: 'No, you are a king.'

Omar: 'Mmm. You're a king too.'

Harrison(puts his arm round Omar): 'Yup!'

Oni to Omar: 'You're not an angel, you're a king.'

Yomi (mixture of regret and pride in her tone, but a sad face):'They took me off being an angel cos I was naughty.'

Yomi to Omar (teasing tone): 'Good girl, good boy.' (to Harrison) 'You good girl.'

Harrison (cross): 'I not a *girl* (disparaging voice). I'm a boy!'

Omar is told in public by Mrs Jones that he cannot be an angel because he is a boy, and as a boy, he is a king. He persists in saying that he wants to do dancing with the angels, but is not allowed to. Other children tease him, calling him a girl because he wants to perform as an angel. He knows he is a boy, but is reluctant to accept the restriction this is placing on him, so he tries out saying he is a girl. Harrison makes sure Omar knows he has made an error, telling him he is a king, and offering this as evidence that he must be a boy! Harrison rewards Omar with a hug when he appears to accept his proper boy role again. Oni and Yomi reinforce the policing of gender boundaries by teasing Omar and Harrison, and Harrison gets very annoyed at the suggestion that he might be a girl. Yomi reveals that she has had the part of angel taken away from her because she has been a naughty girl, so is not proper angel material. Being a good girl is equated with performing angel in the nativity play. Boys, as kings, get away with more boisterous and loud behaviour, without forfeiting their parts in the play.

Reinforcing gender dualism – embodying good school pupil

I followed two cohorts of children as they moved from Nursery to Reception at Ash Vale. In the Reception class knowledge of being a school pupil was much more important in lesson times than knowledge of feminine and masculine markers. However, the children's knowledge of masculinity and femininity practices remained a central feature of boys' and girls' social relations. Being a successful Reception pupil involved keeping the class rules and following instructions and routines, often in public. The children were required to sit on the carpet for several teaching sessions each day and were encouraged to embody good school pupil by sitting up straight, with hands folded, legs crossed, and sometimes fingers on lips to show they were listening quietly. They were encouraged to be quiet and careful when walking and moving around. Nursery routines had prepared them for this. All the children I observed sought and valued positive attention and praise from their teacher.

Although the attributes of good pupil were not gendered, there was a shared assumption by staff and children that boys are different from girls. Most children sat on the carpet with someone of their own sex whenever they could. Despite their eagerness to perform good pupil I saw many same-sex social exchanges on the carpet, many of them non-verbal, as in these fieldnotes:

> All sit very quiet on carpet, no noticeable girl/boy divide, although when I look closely, I can see that girls are sitting with girls, and boys with boys, as usual. Nadia and Molly are having a 'conversation' , they are looking at gap between them, keep on moving to sit closer together, making eye contact, copying each other's gestures, fingers on lips, nothing spoken aloud.
>
> ...
>
> Daniel and Omar sit close together. Omar leans towards Daniel, making eye contact. Daniel smiles and gives Omar a playful punch on the shoulder.

When given the choice, most children opted to work with a same-sex partner in activities on the carpet. This was easier, as they usually sat next to somebody of the same sex, so had only to turn towards them.

> Songs, 'Row the Boat'
>
> Ms Foster: 'Everybody sit with a partner.' Boys all choose another boy, girls another girl, except Lan and Jason who are sitting next to each other and work together.

Although Ms Foster made no overt distinction between the behaviour she expected from boys and girls, and although she gave all children turns to perform every school pupil task, my data shows three times as many instances of girls compared to boys showing knowledge of what it is to be a school pupil. The most frequent exchanges between children in play and group learning situations employed instructional language, issuing commands and admonitions to each other, reflecting the dominant mode of teacher instruction used in the setting. Established children seized opportunities to demonstrate their understanding of class rules and positioned themselves as knowledgeable by instructing children who were unfamiliar with school routines. Girls adopted teacher-like behaviour and issued commands far more often than boys.

Ms Foster made frequent comments about girls' need to modify their appearance, dress and bodily postures, but few about the boys' appearances.

> *Carpet*
>
> Ms Foster: 'Molly, tuck your hair behind your ear.'
>
> ...

Ms Foster to Alita: 'Why did you take down your hair again? We need to keep our hair up all the time, it keeps it from getting knotty and it keeps it clean.'

...

'Molly, pull your skirt down.' (Very short skirt over tights, skirt has ridden up as she walks to get her coat, and Ms Foster notices).

Although all the children were keen to perform jobs around the classroom and all helped with the clearing up, certain girls were often chosen to do more demanding tasks as the girls generally did them more competently. Some of the boys enjoyed showing off their strength and willingness to do jobs, but actually accomplished very little.

Ms Kent: 'Can you please take in the blocks' (general to children in outdoor area).

Ravi: 'I'm strong' (spends ages trying to pick up several blocks at once and trying to carry too many. Making a big deal about it, showing his muscles).

Ms Foster: 'Ravi, Liam, one at a time!'

Liam: 'I want to take that one.'

Jason: 'I'm stronger.'

Jason to Chloe: 'I'm stronger' (shows her he is carrying two blocks to her one).

Perhaps the girls' relative competence influenced the teacher's choice – when she needed something done, it was efficient to choose a sensible girl.

Walkerdine (1990) notes that the only position available to girls in the class-room is often quasi-teacher. Francis (1998, 2000) found that girls in primary and secondary schools frequently positioned themselves as quasi-teacher, adopting 'sensible' behaviour in contrast to boys' 'silliness'. Francis argues that children's constructions of gender as oppositional has an impact on gendered power relations. Some girls believe that their sensible behaviour will gain approval from teachers and other pupils, but some boys take advantage of girls' sensible behaviour to dominate girls and other boys. Francis observed how '...a dominant construction of boys as irresponsible and competitive allowed many boys to dominate the classroom space and interaction, and to exercise power over girls and other boys' (Francis, 2000: 65). Boys in Ash Vale learned that they could gain power and pleasure by dominating other children by taking up selfish positions as opposed to the girls' sensible positions.

The Reception teacher, Ms Foster, allocated the children to one of five ability groups, and they were expected to work in these groups for the majority of lesson times. She decided who would be in each ability group according to the baseline tests from Nursery. In the second year of my research there were ten boys and ten girls in Reception class in the Autumn term. The ability groups were all mixed, ensuring that boys and girls worked together. This underlined the separation of work and play: work happened in ability groups and play happened in single-sex groups. As in Nursery, when there was a chance for free play in Reception, boys and girls separated and played in same sex groups in different spaces. And grouping children by ability created a hierarchy of learning which affected social relations. Below, the 'top' purple group are doing a task at the writing table.

> Ms S directs 'top' purple group to writing table.
>
> ...
>
> Daniel and Ellie, Richard and Jala, sitting together, discussing their letters.
>
> Daniel to Ellie: 'Look at this! I did a big one.'
>
> Ellie to Daniel: '*I* did a big one.'
>
> Oni comes over and looks at Jala's work.
>
> Jala: 'This is a sharp pencil. I'm already finished. Look Oni!'
>
> Daniel: 'Me too! Look at mine!'

There is an undercurrent of competition in the children's interactions, and they are aware that the teacher sees them as the cleverest children and expects them to do more difficult work than their peers. Daniel would not choose to go to the writing table but concentrates with good effect in this directed task.

Ms Foster encouraged the girls in the work groups to be sensible and helpful – not naughty like the boys.

> Teacher calls for purple group (top ability group).
>
> Jala comes out into playground.
>
> Jala (teacher voice, very assertive): 'Daniel, Richard, you gotta come now!'
>
> Richard to Fatima: 'I gotta go. Don't touch my motor'
>
> Fatima: 'OK.'
>
> Richard and Daniel go inside.
>
> After two minutes Richard comes out again, rides bike.

Jala comes out, stands in doorway and calls across to Richard: 'Come *on* Richard! Miss is waiting!'

Richard goes inside again.

(Ms Foster has twice used Jala as a 'sensible' girl to go and fetch Richard. I have noticed that Jala is beginning to be given quite a lot of little jobs like this, as she can be relied on to be sensible and is confident and assertive.)

Ms Foster encouraged the established group of Reception children to enact the correct practices of a Reception child to the Nursery children, thus unwittingly reinforcing gender dualism. Nursery children made several visits to Reception class during the term before they joined the Reception class. In this phonics session, Ms Foster encourages Reception children to show Nursery children what to do.

Phonics on carpet. Children have to outline letters in air, as if they are a robot writing.

Ms Foster 'Stand up if you have a picture of a van.

Show the Nursery how we do it. Get your robot arms ready. VAN!'

... Ms Foster: 'Have any of you Nursery children got a web? *Web!* (to Reception) Show them the picture of the web so they know what it looks like.'

Alita: 'He got one!' (indicating Leon)

Fifi looking worried.

Ms Foster: 'Reception can you show the Nursery how we do strong robot arms to say ZIP?'

Extra keen rendering of the robot arms.

At the end of the session, the teacher invited Reception children to take care of a Nursery child for the next play session. She did not suggest same-sex pairs, but all the children picked somebody of the same sex. The girls all went to the writing area, the boys to the construction area.

Ms Foster: 'Now you can all go and choose an activity. I am looking to see who is sitting nicely to go and choose. Melek, you pick someone from Nursery and go with them.'

Melek picks Eser, holds her hand, takes her to writing area.

Tagan picks Fifi, takes her to join Melek and Eser.

Oni picks Tia and joins the other girls.

Oni and Tia talking quietly together colouring in pics.

In turn, Tu, Ben and Jake pick Ervin, Adil and Leon and take them to the construction area.

Thus the teacher encouraged established children to induct newcomers into Reception practices of femininity and masculinity. New children immediately began to participate as peripheral members, learning that it is usual for girls and boys to play separately, as they did in Nursery.

Children, too, seized opportunities to reinforce gender dualism. In the following Reception class PE lesson, girls and boys sit in same-sex couples and groups when given a choice, making eye contact, laughing and gesturing to each other. The teacher does not intend to set up a competitive atmosphere between boys and girls, but as soon as she differentiates, children seize on an oppositional interpretation of gender difference. Omar does not like it when the teacher praises the girls' performances.

PE in Hall

Children jump and hop along their ropes.

Ms Daly: 'Right, girls all sit down, boys stay standing.'

'Boys, show the girls what you have been doing.'

Boys demonstrate.

Ms Daly: 'Good work. Now boys sit down and girls stand up. Show the boys what you have been doing.'

Girls demonstrate.

Ms Daly: 'Well done, look at their concentration boys!'

Omar (singsong chanting voice): 'Girls are losing!'

Other boys join in the chant.

Ms Daly (sounds annoyed): 'It's not about winning or losing.'

Even when staff were careful to avoid being sexist, the children at Ash Vale often behaved in gendered ways, as in the following episode. Four girls volunteer to carry trays of toys, enacting sensible helpful behaviour. The teacher tries to avoid being sexist by encouraging boys as well as girls to carry the toys but the boys opt out.

Nursery garden

Mrs Teal gets some children to carry in some of the trays of toys, as it looks as though it is going to rain. She asks for 'strong people', but none of the boys respond. They go on playing ball.

Mrs Teal: 'I need some strong people to carry these in.'

Four girls rush to help. Some quarrelling amongst the girls about who is going to carry the trays.

Yomi to Melek: 'You took mine!' (accusing, angry voice)

Ayo (to Mrs Teal): 'I'm strong!'

Mrs Teal (smiling approvingly): 'Yes, you eat your dinner up.' (Four girls carry in the trays. No boys show any interest in helping).

Mrs Teal does not ask any boys to help, so the implicit message is that boys are free to go on playing whilst the girls clear up, although the official rule is that all children help clear away. She thinks it would be sexist to ask boys rather than girls to carry things, but the effect is to allow the girls full responsibility for the clearing up.

Implications for early childhood teaching and research

Newcomers to Ash Vale's early years classes learned from established classmates that some activities and spaces were for girls and some for boys. They policed each others' play very strictly. To be accepted into play activities, the children had to show that they knew that boys and girls had separate spheres. Boys learned to dominate spaces and perform practices of hegemonic masculinity in battle games, football and construction activities, and girls learned practices of emphasised femininity, often bolstering boys' power at their own expense, but also resisting boys' domination of space.

Early years practitioners and researchers need to be aware that young children learn gendered play by observing older children. It is not enough to tell children that all activities are open to boys and girls alike. We need to intervene in children's play and encourage children to question and discuss their play choices. When young children cross gender borders, we need to recognise what they are doing and understand how difficult it is for them to so. Support from adults in early years settings is crucial to the success of children's efforts to resist stereotypical gender play.

Checklist for action for gender equity

■ Monitor the play in your setting on a regular basis. Note who uses the construction areas, roleplay areas, writing, IT and book areas. Note who dominates play in the different areas at different times. Who takes control and how do they achieve domination? Who is excluded and why? Discuss this with colleagues and with the children.

■ Encourage children to talk about the ways gender relates to race and ethnicity, and ability. Focus on issues of gender equity in all stages of curriculum planning and delivery and celebrate and make use of the children's home languages and rich cultural experiences. For example involve parents and grandparents in history, music and language projects in school.

■ Develop strategies for enabling all children to get access to space, resources and equipment. Consider introducing timed periods of play and girls' only periods for access to certain play spaces and equipment. Introduce a system that makes it possible for children to choose an activity in advance eg put down their names for construction activities.

■ Provide opportunities for children to work collaboratively and co-operatively in same-sex and mixed groups as this can develop young children's ability to position themselves in ways that challenge gender dualism. Introduce a variety of work groupings and avoid a gendered separation of work and play.

■ Actively support children who try to cross gender boundaries in their play. Provide role models of gender equity in stories. Intervene in play to enable children to experience pleasure and power in activities that involve crossing gender borders eg boys bathing dolls, girls with construction toys.

■ Do not reinforce gender dualism by suggesting that it is natural for boys and girls to play at different activities or behave in different ways.

■ Avoid allocating parts in games and drama that are stereotypically gendered eg girls as the princesses or angels and boys the princes or warriors.

■ Be aware of the discourse of 'sensible girls' versus 'silly boys'. Do not reinforce this by choosing sensible girls to do jobs, however tempting this is!

■ Remember that children experience huge pressures to conform to gendered play and do not be surprised or discouraged if your interventions seem to make little difference. Persevere – you are offering important alternatives that could benefit the children for the rest of their lives.

5

Imaginative and socio-dramatic play

This chapter explores how children who were new in Ash Vale early years classes learned to take gendered roles in imaginative and socio-dramatic play. New boys watched older boys and learned to take part in superhero and 'battle' play. New girls watched older girls and learned to take part in play scenarios that centred on home life and fairy tales. Boys and girls did sometimes play together, usually taking gendered roles. They developed story lines about school and family life and played chasing games. Power relations between the children were important in shaping their imaginative play. Some children learned to dominate particular spaces by claiming them for boys or for girls.

Both boys and girls strictly policed imaginative play activities, often insisting that certain dressing up clothes, roles and behaviours were only for girls or only for boys. Older boys and girls used their understanding of masculine and feminine activities to dominate other children and seize moments of power. For example, girls experienced power in the role of mother and teacher, and boys experienced power as superheroes. Some children could successfully border cross in their imaginative play.

The roleplay areas are for girls?

The staff in Ash Vale early years classes told the children that everyone, girls and boys, could enjoy the roleplay areas, and staff encouraged all children to take part in a range of imaginative play. Nursery and Reception classes had roleplay areas indoors and outdoors. Children who were new in Nursery and Reception often chose to play in the roleplay areas. But they soon learned from other children that there were gender rules about who could play in these areas. Domestic socio-dramatic play was a key feminine play practice in Ash Vale. Girls usually, but not always, dominated the roleplay areas. As we saw in Chapter 4, roleplay areas and writing areas were often the only places where girls could play without boys disrupting their games. Girls seized moments of power and control in these spaces.

Girls who were new to Nursery often copied aspects of older girls' play. In the following play sequence, we see Fifi, here in her first term at Nursery, learning from older girls.

Nursery garden

Tagan and Oni go into the playhouse, get dolls, put them in buggies and push them round the area outside the play house. Fifi standing watching them. Fifi goes into the playhouse, puts a doll in a buggy and follows Oni and Tagan round, pushing her buggy.

Mrs Jones: 'Oh very good Fifi, you've got a baby in your buggy.'

Fifi smiles.

Thus Fifi is learning that adults in Nursery approve of girls who push dolls around in buggies. She embodies feminine girl behaviour. By pushing the doll in the pram with other girls, she begins to take part in a central play practice of girls in this Nursery community of femininity. The older girls allow her to follow them but do not include her in their roleplay. Fifi observed and copied aspects of older girls' play, and this was an important stage in her learning about appropriate feminine play in the Nursery. Gradually, older girls Tagan and Oni allowed Fifi to take an active part in co-operative socio-dramatic play with dolls and buggies.

Girls often experienced moments of power through taking up the role of mother, teacher and fairy tale princess. In the next play sequence, we see Lan, wearing a pink Barbie Dancing Princesses Tshirt and using her knowledge of Disney fairy tale princesses to direct the action in the roleplay area. Although it has been set up by staff as *The House of the Three Bears*, three girls, Lan, Sara and Sammie, introduce a storyline based on their shared knowledge of Disney princesses, and exclude a boy, Mani. Mani, the only full-time boy in this term's Nursery class, tries to gain access to the home corner roleplay area, which is dominated by girls. The girls argue about who will take a powerful role in the story. Mani is not as fluent or confident in English as any of these girls. He shows that he has learned some of the rules for being accepted in the roleplay area by the girls, but he has insufficient knowledge and command of Disney princess stories to take a full part in the action, and is there under sufferance. He changes his position from the relatively powerful Daddy bear to powerless baby, but the girls go on ignoring him, and he leaves the area.

Roleplay area set up as 'House of Three Bears' in 'Goldilocks'.

Mani: 'I'm the Daddy Bear'

Lan showing her Barbie Dancing Princesses tshirt to Sammie and Sara, they name the princesses, very animated, ignoring Mani.

Sara: 'I be the Cinderella ... (to Mani) Please can you be quiet!'

Lan: 'I be Jasmine'

...

Lan: 'I'm Cinderella'

Sammie: 'I'm Sleeping Beauty.'

Lan: 'Tomorrow my Mum going to get me Little Mermaid'

Mani: 'I'm be the baby' (girls ignore him).

Mani leaves roleplay area.

...

Sammie to Chloe: 'She (indicating Sara) is the ugly sister.'

Sammie to Sara: 'You said you're the ugly sister so you gotta be'

Sara: 'No!'

Sammie: 'We can't have three princesses otherwise it'll be another story!'

At first sight, it might seem that the girls behaved unkindly towards Mani. As a teacher, you might want to encourage the girls to include Mani in their play. However, the context of this play is important. The roleplay area in this classroom was one of the only spaces where girls could play without encountering disruptive behaviour from boys. Space and play activity in Ash Vale were linked to power struggles. Girls took power in the roleplay area, as it was usually the only space they could control.

Sometimes girls could not gain access even to the roleplay space. During the third term of my research a group of older boys took control of any area of the Nursery they decided to play in. There were 30 part-time children, of whom ten were boys and twenty were girls in Nursery this term but eight boys and only two girls were full-timers. Some of the older full-time boys learned to dominate space and activities in all the play areas. The children's gendered use of indoor and outdoor spaces during this term is shown in Plans C and D overleaf.

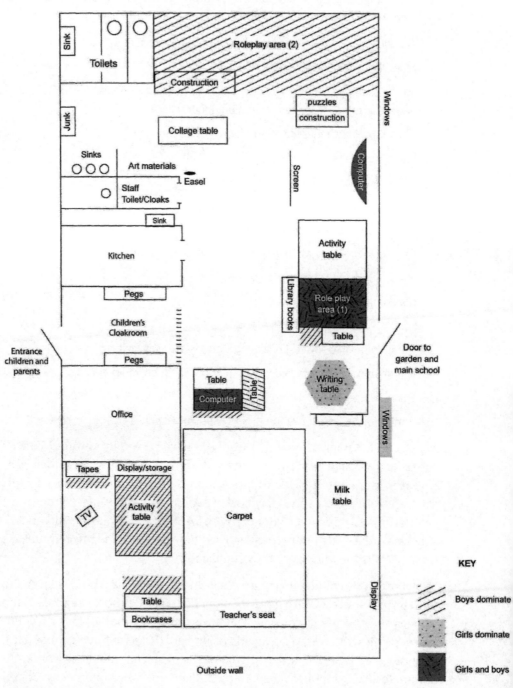

Plan C
Nursery Classroom

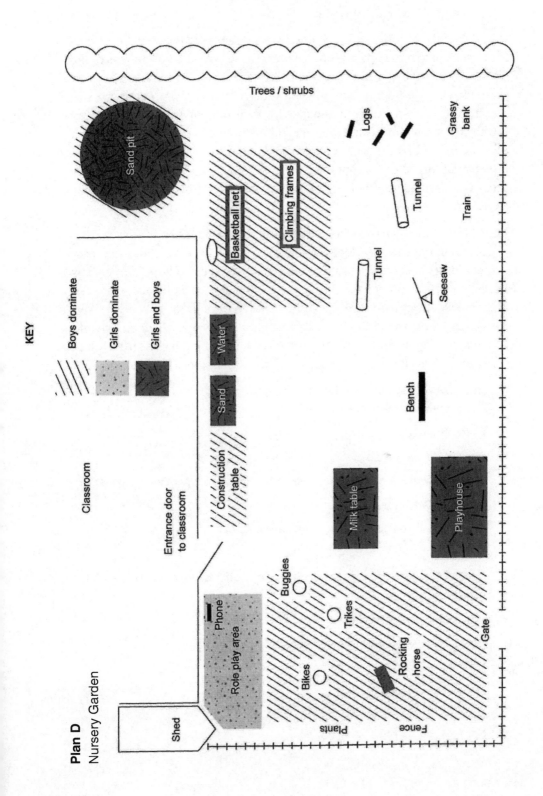

Plan D
Nursery Garden

KEY

Boys dominate

Girls dominate

Girls and boys

Trees / shrubs

Sand pit

Logs

Grassy bank

Tunnel

Train

Basketball net

Climbing frames

Tunnel

Seesaw

Classroom

Water

Sand

Entrance door to classroom

Construction table

Bench

Milk table

Playhouse

Shed

Phone

Role play area

Buggies

Trikes

Bikes

Rocking horse

Plants

Fence

Gate

Daniel, Jake, Harrison, Ben, Lewis and Ryan often played together. Ervin, new to Nursery, began to copy their behaviour. These boys took over areas of the classroom and playground by combining together and using their physical presence and loud comments to keep other children away. Outdoors, this group controlled space round the gate for their football games. Girls played mostly in the play house and area around the phone. Girls sometimes linked arms and marched round the playground chanting 'Here come the girls!' I understand this as an attempt to claim some space for themselves in a situation where a small group of older boys had taken control of most of the play areas.

Daniel and Harrison, who were particularly skilled at strategies of exclusion, took leading roles in the older boys' games. These boys were also the most competent speakers of English that term. In the next episode we can see how Daniel and Harrison are able to use their competence as English speakers, their knowledge of Nursery rules (four only at a time in roleplay areas), and their combined physical force to implement a strategy that excluded girls and younger children from the roleplay area. They acted together assertively and confidently, and claimed all the space in the roleplay area.

> Ryan, Daniel, Harrison and Ben in roleplay area, which is set up as a Chinese restaurant for Chinese New Year.
>
> Ryan: 'Where the food gone?'
>
> Daniel: 'We need shooters'
>
> (Boys are pointing chopsticks at each other, and using them as weapons)
>
> Zoe at the entrance, looking on.
>
> Daniel: (gently but firmly to her) 'You can't come in!'
>
> Malik comes over to entrance.
>
> Daniel: 'Zoe, you can't come in. Malik, you can't come in. (to Harrison) I'm gonna stay here and not let anyone in'
>
> Malik goes away, chewing his finger disconsolately.
>
> Zoe goes on watching from entrance.
>
> Malik comes back to the entrance.
>
> Daniel: (warningly) 'Malik!'
>
> Harrison (loudly): '1, 2, 3, 4!' (ie it's full in here.)
>
> Mrs Clarke calls Daniel to work with her.

As he leaves the area, Daniel calls to Harrison: 'Don't let anyone in but me. You stay!'

Malik tries to get in again, Ervin also comes over and makes as if to enter.

Harrison: 'You can't go in!'

Harrison: 'Ben, just keep in!'

Harrison stands with one arm on each side of the entrance, blocking it, and barring anybody from entering, although there are only three children in there.

The early years staff shared with me their concern that the group of older boys were so dominant. Staff set up a new roleplay area, a fire station, in the space that was previously the construction area. They wanted to encourage boys to take part in roleplay and let younger children have a turn in domestic role-play. This new roleplay area immediately became very popular with many boys because of the fire helmets and firefighter equipment. Boys enjoyed battle games in this area and frequently claimed the area for boys. In the following episode, Ervin, a new boy this term, joins in with Tu and Lewis, old-timers, to exclude Jala and Tagan, two of the older girls.

Lewis, Tu and Ervin playing in fire station role play area.

Tagan on edge of area, hands on hips, looks determined, makes loud announcement 'I gonna come in!'

Lewis: (loudly) ' Na! 1,2,3,4' (as if, there's four already, but actually there are only three).

Tu: '*You* can't come in. You a *girl.*'

Tagan: (defiantly) 'I'm a girl!' (as if, so what!)

Tu: (chanting, jumping around and laughing at her) 'I'm a girl, I'm a girl, I'm a cake!'

Tagan points to him, smiling, still standing on edge of mat 'You're a boy!'

Tagan: 'I want to come in.'

Jala comes over and stands beside her.

Ervin: (warningly)'1,2,3,4,5,6,'

Jala (makes as if to enter): '1,2,3,4,5,6,7.'

Boys taking up lots of space, leaping about and making lots of noise, menacing Jala and Tagan and blocking the entrance to the area.

Jala and Tagan leave area.

The boys used the rule of four only to keep out the girls, then they made a lot of noise and used physical gestures to back up the verbal refusal. This makes it sound more deliberate than it probably was, as their usual play style was noisy and expansive. But it also served to exclude the girls. Tu also used humour and teasing to exclude Tagan. Tagan understood that she was being excluded because she was a girl. She was at a further disadvantage because she could not count to four, and was not sure whether there were already four in the roleplay area. Jala was confident with numbers to ten and ignored the four only rule, but she still failed to gain access.

When staff realised that these boys were dominating the new roleplay area, they were dismayed, but concluded 'that's just how boys are – naturally boisterous.' Discourses of gender dualism and developmentally appropriate practice encourage early years teachers think it wrong to intervene in young children's play, and this belief makes it difficult for them to pursue gender equity. When the boys excluded Tagan and Jala, a more proactive strategy would have been to talk to the children about what was happening and perhaps set up a girls' only time in the new roleplay area.

Battle games are for boys?

Boys in the Nursery classes learned to take part in battles and associated superhero play. Some developed superhero play themes, often taken from films such as *Spiderman* and *Power Rangers,* and showed their physical strength, competitiveness and comradeship through elaborate displays of wrestling, running and leaping around the playground. At lunch play many of the boys in Reception classes put up the hoods on their coats and wore them open, like capes, to be superhero costumes, as they engaged in territorial playground battles. They ran back and forth between the two playgrounds, and had wrestling bouts against the walls and on the grassy bank, out of sight of the lunchtime supervisors. Younger boys would often run after older boys, copying their gestures. I saw boys getting hurt in these battle games.

I use the term 'battle play' to describe the fighting games, because this is what the boys themselves often called it, and it emphasises the serious strategic work that took place in these games. To take a full part in battle games, boys had to develop physical skills in running, jumping, bodily strength and en-durance, and knowledge of superhero storylines.

I saw all the boys in Ash Vale early years classes actively position themselves as participants in battle play, although some did so more than others. Some, such as Omar, did not participate at first but gradually got drawn in. In the following play episode we see Omar watching a battle game. He does not join in, and reports the boys who are playing it to a staff member. This earns him a hostile reaction from Daniel.

> *Ryan, Daniel, Harrison, Jake, playing a very energetic superhero game, involving chasing and capturing each other across the Nursery play area and onto the climbing frame. Very expansive gestures, loud cries and having lots of fun.*
>
> Omar not joining in, watching them, on his own, going round on scooter.
>
> Daniel: 'Stretch rangers!' (arms out, runs up and climbs to top of climbing frame.)
>
> Omar to Mrs Teal: 'They are playing the sword game.'
>
> Mrs Teal: 'Oh I hope not, we don't want anybody getting hurt.'
>
> Daniel(hostile look at Omar): 'No, we're not!'

Omar was very keen to play with Daniel and realised that he would have to join in battle play if he wanted to develop a friendship with him. Over the next months I often saw Omar practising the physical moves he would need, and taking an increasingly active part in boys' battle games.

Boys who were not particularly athletic had to persevere with determination to gain acceptance to the battle play. Tu worked hard for the whole time he was in Nursery, and it was only in the Reception class that he really became established as a full member of the boys' community of practice of masculinity. He achieved acceptance partly by persevering in football. As he became more confident in English, Tu was able to take a more active part in developing plots in battle games, and used his sense of humour to amuse other boys.

> *Ryan and Tu in construction area*
>
> Ryan crouching down, firing 'gun'.
>
> Tu follows, pointing and shooting two guns: 'OOO piu, piu.'
>
> Tu: 'The monster coming!'
>
> Tu points gun up at ceiling: 'I missed it!'
>
> Ryan (laughing): 'Look Tu, piu, piu!'

Early years staff discouraged battle play, but this disapproval sometimes seemed to make the activity more attractive. The disapproval of [female] adults gave extra excitement to the battle play, as the boys enjoyed evading the watchful eye of the lunchtime supervisors and teachers. Staff, particularly at lunchtime, did not notice all the battle games and I saw some boys getting hurt. However, most of the battle moves were very stylised, designed as public displays, and not intended to hurt anybody. Certainly, I saw many power struggles between individuals and groups of boys, but these mostly revolved around who was leading and directing the battles rather than physical fights in a combative sense. In the next episode we see Daniel and Harrison both trying to direct the action.

> *Nursery Garden.* Daniel, Jake, Harrison and Ryan on climbing frame.
>
> Daniel (On top of climbing frame): 'Oh no, there's an emergency, come on!'
>
> Jake joins Daniel, shouting: 'Everyone! Save the world!'
>
> Ryan: 'Daniel and Jake!'
>
> Harrison: 'No! You come up to the ship. I'm the baddies!'
>
> Mrs Teal: 'Boys, not that fast running' (pleasant tone, and they don't take any notice).

Many of the narratives centred on such archetypal themes of goodies and baddies. The teacher mildly rebukes the boys for running, as it is against the rules in the Nursery garden. But she does not remark on the fact that these boys are taking up all the space in the play area. Girls seldom tried to take part in these games, and on the rare occasion they did, their bodies appeared un-accustomed to performing in ways that enabled them to participate, and those who wore short tight skirts were prevented from moving easily. This is not to say that girls would not move as freely as the boys if they habitually took part in such play. In the episode below, Tagan, unusually, gets involved in a battle play, but soon retreats to the playhouse.

> Tagan, Jake, Ben, Ryan, Omar in wild chasing game round play area, all very animated. Turns into play fighting, when Tagan pushes Ben. Jake starts doing karate kicks, fists out, shadow boxing. Ben and Omar join in similar actions.
>
> Ben fists up, against Omar.
>
> Tagan (wearing a tight skirt) trying karate type kicks, but looks uncomfortable. Moves away to playhouse.

Early years staff tended to intervene if they thought play appeared to be getting too rough or likely to injure anybody. Boys tried to avoid staff seeing their battle games, but often wanted their performances to be seen by other boys. The adult disapproval of one major form of hegemonic masculinity in Ash Vale early years classes has implications for how young boys developed gender identities. Female staff disapproved of battle play and often discouraged or actively forbade it. In the following exchange, Daniel and Omar talk about the details of a wrestling programme they saw on TV. At the same time, Daniel takes the opportunity to assure Omar that he will beat up a boy in another class who Omar says has been attacking him.

> Madison, Omar and Daniel at playdough table, discussing wrestling.
>
> Omar (looks upset) (to Daniel): 'Tarak got me. It was Tarak.'
>
> Daniel (puts arm round him): 'I'll beat him up for you. You know John Michael he's the champion.'
>
> Ms Foster overhears, comes over, asks what they are talking about.
>
> Daniel: 'Wrestling, I saw it on the TV.'
>
> Ms Foster: 'Wrestling? On TV? Oh, OK.'
>
> Ms Foster goes away.
>
> Daniel: 'Then he kicked him down. He was on the rope and Batista kicked him down. He got him and then he kicked him.'
>
> Omar (grinning): 'Yeah, he kicked him down.'

Daniel positions himself as a hero, supporting his friend, by offering to beat up Tarak. Daniel realises that Ms Foster would not approve of this and says they are talking about wrestling. Ms Foster appears reassured by this response, and leaves them to continue their talk. This emphasises the ambiguities of adults' position on fighting in the classroom. Talking about wrestling is acceptable because it is an official sport: wrestling in the classroom or playground is definitely not, because it might result in injury. But the emotional pleasure Omar and Daniel appear to feel from the exchange seems to be about giving themselves feelings of being powerful, through narrating a story about fighting, identifying themselves with the successful wrestlers. Madison is sitting with them, but makes no contribution to the conversation.

Some girls positioned themselves as quasi-teachers and gained pleasure from threatening to tell staff when boys were engaging in battle play. Sometimes girls did report the boys' transgression but more often they used the threat to gain a feeling that they were powerful, and good, in contrast to boys' badness.

> Amena to BM: 'That's the battle table (pointing to group of boys engaged in a shooting game with stickle bricks). If I tell miss, they'll get in trouble.'

I understand this in the context of 'spirals of power and pleasure' (Foucault, 1976), whereby the girls gained pleasure from detecting and exposing the boys' wrongdoing, and the boys enjoyed evading detection Francis' (1998) research with older primary school children documented many instances of boys 'silliness' contrasting with girls' 'sensible' behaviour, and she shows how this emphasised gender difference. In Ash Vale, children learned to take up oppositional gender positions through their attitudes to battle play.

Liam talked to me one lunch time about his ambivalent feelings about battle games. He was in his second term in Reception at this time.

I am sketching groups of children in play areas at lunch time.

Liam to BM: 'What are you drawing?'

BM: 'I'm drawing a picture of your playground.'

Liam: 'Why have you drawn me?'

BM: 'Well, it isn't you, but I will draw you if you want me to.'

Liam: 'Can I draw in your book?'

I give the book to Liam and he draws a picture of himself skipping, and one of a girl walking to the flower bed.

BM: 'That's a great picture. Do you like to skip Liam?'

Liam: 'Yes, at home. Not here.'

Liam (points to his picture of a girl): 'I would like to play with her. I don't know her name. But that boy, he (Liam points to a Year 1 boy) always fights me.'

BM: 'Why does he do that?'

Liam (disapprovingly): 'I think he watches Power Rangers. It makes you a bit fighty.'

BM: 'Do you like to fight?'

Liam: 'No! (excited) I like to jump on people's heads!'

...

Later in this lunch play, Liam comes running up to me.

Liam (to BM, very excited): 'I'm doing battles!'

On one level, Liam was excited by the battles. I imagine that he has been told, possibly at home, that watching Power Ranger films can make you behave aggressively, and he is both disapproving and at the same time eager to join in. I saw Liam getting hurt several times in playground battles, once having his arm twisted, and being wrestled to the ground, and he did not appear to be enjoying himself but persevered in joining these games. Liam was learning that taking part in battles was an important way of demonstrating member-ship of the community of practice of boys in the playground. He saw that his knowledge and enjoyment of skipping were not appropriate for lunchtime play in this playground culture. He confessed to me privately that he would like to play with a girl, but I never saw him try to do so. Liam's experience emphasises for me how difficult it was for boys in this setting to resist identifying themselves with practices of hegemonic masculinity.

My position as adult female researcher made my observations of battle play problematic. I was often poised to intervene if battles seemed to me to be too rough, and boys often stopped their games if I was nearby. My own attitude to these games was ambivalent, and I expect this was apparent to the boys. Interestingly, most boys were reluctant to talk to me about their battle play, and no one wanted to tell me about it in the interviews about playtime, although they were keen to tell me about football. I conclude that they felt this was an area of expertise that was the preserve of boys, and, as a female and a disapproving adult, I was excluded. This was in marked contrast to the occasion in Reception class when the boys all seemed to enjoy playing with the capes I took in, and developed storylines around rescues, on themes of animals, birds and space. However, they differentiated this play from their own battle play. On one occasion I observed Daniel taking off his cape before engaging in a battle game.

Swain (2003) describes how 10 year-old boys learn to embody a range of hegemonic masculine practices, arguing that 'The body is thus an integral part of identity and of our biographies, for the process of making and becoming a body also involves the project of making the self' (p300). The boys in Ash Vale learned to value certain masculine performances, and fashion their bodies in specific ways so as to position themselves as strong in relation to other boys, and superior to girls. Boys in Ash Vale used their battle games to embody and explore aspects of hegemonic masculinity, drawing on discourses that circulate beyond the school, in media images and home communities. My findings add to work of Jordan (1995), Marsh (2000) and Browne (2004), who report that young boys use superhero play to position themselves as powerful through enacting a warrior discourse, drawing on images of fictional male superheroes.

Boys and girls together

The children in Ash Vale learned to take part in imaginative play that emphasised gender differences and many of the play episodes where girls and boys played together involved spirals of pleasure and power. Same-sex play episodes also involved spirals of pleasure and power, as in the episode when girls use knowledge of Disney fairytale stories to gain the upper hand over each other (see p95). However, same-sex power struggles usually lacked the oppositional confrontational aspects I found in scenes when boys and girls were together.

In the following episode, we see Daniel, Melek and Jake playing schools in the roleplay area in their first term in Reception. Melek takes power in the role of female teacher, and the two boys resist her authority. This scenario was a popular play theme, and often ended, as in this case, with naughty boys getting the upper hand. The children are acting out school routines that are familiar to them, but they introduce their own power relations within the play scenes. Here, Daniel and Jake enjoyed being disobedient in ways they would never be with their teacher. Melek uses her position as teacher to exercise control, and she introduces the pink handbag to undermine Daniel's menacing behaviour with the gorilla.

Roleplay area

Daniel comes in.

Daniel: 'Let's play school.'

Melek: 'OK we play school.'

Daniel sits down on chair, Melek sits opposite him, on 'teacher's chair'.

Melek starts reading a book in a teacherly voice.

Daniel starts being naughty, fidgeting, then grabs the book.

Melek: 'No! Give that to me!'

A tussle with the book.

Melek: 'I'm goin to do the register now!'

Daniel: 'Look, you see this?' (points to a picture in the book.)

Melek: 'Mm. OK now sit down *now.*'

Daniel sits down.

Melek starts ticking names on piece of paper.

Melek: 'Right, come and get the register!'

Daniel stands.

Melek: 'OK. Put the register in here!' (indicates the table)

Jake comes in, sits on a chair next to Daniel.

Melek (sits back on teacher chair, holding a piece of paper, looking at boys to see if they are ready, stern expression, as if 'I'm waiting for you to be sitting properly'): 'OK now!'

Jake smiling, sitting up very straight with arms folded, exaggerated pose of 'good pupil'.

Melek: 'OK!' (looks at her piece of paper)

Daniel gets up starts playing with the soft toys, gets the gorilla and makes it jump up and down in front of Melek. Jake joins in, waving his arms in front of Melek.

Melek:'No!'

Enter Richard (new boy) watching them.

Melek snatches the gorilla from Daniel, grabs a pink handbag off the shelf.

To Daniel: 'And *you* get the handbag!'

Daniel looks very fed up, face screwed up in a grimace of disgust 'No, oh! (as in no way!) 'That's a girls' one!'

Daniel grabs the gorilla and menaces Melek.

Melek leaves roleplay area.

In this last exchange Melek uses her knowledge that boys consider pink a pollutant, annoying Daniel by offering him a pink handbag. Daniel and Jake use physical gestures to overpower Melek. The children enjoy this school game and through their play they emphasise gender difference.

Policing gender boundaries in imaginative play

There were racks of dressing up clothes in the Nursery and Reception classes. These included a variety of hats and tabards and specific items such as equipment for a hospital and a fire station. In both Nursery and Reception, children policed the roleplay clothes strictly, insisting that girls were not allowed to wear firefighters', footballers' or builders' outfits, and boys were not to wear dresses. Boys were ridiculed if they wore or played with anything pink.

The colour pink was reified (Wenger, 1998; Paechter, 2003a) as a symbol for girl things. It was used inclusively by girls, and seen by boys as a pollutant or sign of feminine weakness. Below, Mani offers to share his sand bucket with another boy, Ravi, to save Ravi from being contaminated by a pink bucket.

Sand tray

Ravi starts to fill a pink bucket with sand.

Mani (to Ravi, urgent voice): 'No! You can't have that. That's for girls. Pink! You can share my one.'

In the following episode Harrison extends the category of pink for girls into dinosaur play, in an attempt to exercise power over Chloe. His performance is successful because she changes her position from performing fierce dinosaur to female in need of protection, and abandons the game.

Nursery. Small world play with dinosaurs.

Chloe and Harrison

Chloe to Harrison (advancing a dinosaur to attack his dinosaur, roaring fiercely): 'Rah, rhah'

Harrison to Chloe (scornful):'You don't even scare me.' Gives her a pink dinosaur. 'You gotta have this one. It's a girl one.' Attacks her dinosaur 'Mrrr, rrh' (fierce sounds)

Chloe (high pitched voice): 'Help!'

Shona comes and sits next to Chloe, they do not play with the dinosaurs, talk together, leaning towards each other, giggles, eye contact.

For many boys, pink is to be avoided at all costs. Researchers including Ivinson and Murphy (2007) have documented how some boys will go to considerable lengths to avoid anything pink, such as refusing to use pink paint in their portraits. Douglas (1966) argues that although pollution can be committed intentionally, intention is irrelevant to its effect, and pollution is usually unintentional. The result of becoming polluted is that a polluting person unleashes danger for others because they have crossed some line or developed a wrong condition (Douglas, 1966). This is what happened when young boys treated pink objects as pollutants in Ash Vale Nursery. Pink is understood to feminise and therefore weaken boys. In order to stay strong and protected as a group, they needed to avoid this symbol of femininity (Martin, 2010).

Oppositional gender work – policing the boundaries

Borders frequently require people to identify which side they are on, emphasising differences rather than similarities. They are used in disputes over territory, resources and ideologies. Thorne (1993) uses the metaphor of borders in her analysis of interactions between girls and boys in elementary schools in America. She takes the term from Barth (1969), who uses it in the context of analysis of social relations that are maintained across ethnic boundaries. Thorne cautions against interpreting the image of border as an unyielding fence that divides social relations and replaces it with the image of many short fences that are built up and taken down quickly (Thorne, 1993:

84). This is a useful interpretation as it emphasises that gender boundaries are not fixed and that the salience of gender varies depending upon the situation.

Thorne uses the term 'borderwork' to refer to situations when girls and boys interact with each other in ways that are based upon, and sometimes strengthen, gender boundaries. These situations consist of chasing games, contests, pollution rituals and invasions. She describes the ritual, stylised, scripted quality of many such encounters, and suggests that they are so compelling because they are characterised by intense emotions, forbidden desires, and conflict. These episodes emphasise hegemonic views of gender as oppositional and exaggerate gender differences.

I saw many instances of oppositional encounters between groups of girls and boys, in the Garden area of the Nursery and in the Reception playground. As in the episode below, girls sometimes invoked pink as a symbol for powerful femininity. Girls sometimes seized power at the climbing frame in the Nursery garden. In the following episode, Ayo declares that the climbing frame is a pink house and boys are not allowed. She is using pink in a symbolic, not literal sense, as the climbing frame is yellow. She uses pink as a rallying cry to the girls, as a symbol of female power and feminine solidarity.

> *Ayo, Yomi, Ayla, Molly on the climbing frame.*
>
> Ayo (standing on the climbing frame, speaking loudly, as if making an announcement): 'This is girls' pink house, boys not allowed to come in'
>
> Three more girls run over and get on to the climbing frame, total seven.
>
> Yomi: 'This is a secret place'
>
> Girls chanting loudly, rhythmically, together, hugging close together 'Her, hay, her, hay'.
>
> Daniel and Kumi run over together, in attacking postures, at base of climbing frame, both wearing caps, making loud combative sounds 'Rah, rah', punching air with their fists (playful, with hint of aggression, fists in the air, threatening tone, facial expressions combative) (girls have advantage of height and strength of numbers, plus the solidarity engendered by shared chant). All children involved appear to be enjoying themselves, absorbed in their performances. To me it has the feel of a staged event, a ritual. Unusually, no adults outside.
>
> Ayla climbs into the tunnel.

Ayla:'Ha, ha, ha ha' (chanting, looking out at the boys from inside the tunnel, amused, mischievous grin).

Daniel comes charging up in attacking mode, laughing, fist punching air, holds onto his cap, running round the bottom of climbing frame. Tu (one of youngest boys) running after him, copying him.

When the girls chant together, they link arms and hug, and their physical closeness emphasises their group membership as girls. Ayo and Yomi were often leaders in these ritual power bids, and they derived great pleasure from leading a group of girls and taking over territory on the climbing frame. Younger girls often watched them, and then joined in. A great sense of drama and excitement developed as more girls joined and the volume of the chanting increased. Some of the boys enjoyed responding to the girls' challenges by grouping together and going into battle mode, attacking the girls' stronghold, as in the episode above.

The ritual format of the girls' and boys' different performances here is similar to the playground episodes documented by Thorne (1993). The episodes were an enactment of gender difference and symbolised gender as not only different but oppositional. The girl power bids usually started when adult supervision was at a minimum, as staff discouraged them. Mrs Teal told me that some girls quite often tried to take over on the climbing frames, and I observed similar episodes during the term when a group of older girls were the full-timers in the Nursery, but saw none in the following terms when the full-timers were a group of older boys.

I understand the girl power episodes as taking place in the context of the Nursery where girls had to struggle to gain access to resources and space. The pink girl power bids were successful attempts by the more assertive girls to gain space and control over activities. Girls often had difficulty accessing the climbing frames at other times, as boys routinely excluded and sidelined them. Some boys tried to keep girls off the climbing frames, by demonstrating their superior skills and trying to make the girls take the role of spectator. Consequently the girls had few opportunities to develop their climbing skills. The climbing frames in the Nursery garden were contested territory and were often the scenes of ritual confrontations.

The milk cartons became another focus for ritual borderwork. Reception children were given a carton of milk each day and went to the milk table to drink it when they had finished their work, so this was a time when boys and girls were often together. There were two designs on the cartons. As the classroom

assistant labelled each carton with a child's name before the school day, children had no choice over which carton they got. I presume that the manufacturers intended the 'moohican' carton to appeal to boys because of the masculine hairstyle, and the 'miss spectacular' carton with the bikini top and pink lips to appeal to girls.

The children made their own meanings from the logos, and the designs were the focus of gendered arguments and insults. There was an ongoing debate amongst the children in Reception about girls' and boys' milk, and a particularly common and hurtful insult was to say to another child that they had boy milk if they were a girl, or girl milk if they were a boy. This reflects anxiety about gender constancy but the insults were also used to tease and antagonise members of the opposite sex. The legend of boy and girl milk was passed on through successive groups of children, and the insults often had a ritual quality of repetition and oppositional confrontation.

Milk table

Children are comparing their milk cartons again.

Jake to Ayan (new girl): 'You got boy milk. You're a boy!'

Ayan(standing up): 'I'm telling of him!' (pointing to Jake)

Melek (to Ayan, matter of factly): 'He said I'm a boy too, but I'm not, I'm a girl!'

Ayan moves away from the boys and sits by Melek. Melek smiles at *her*.

When Jake says Ayan has got boy milk so she is a boy, it annoys and upsets her. Melek tells Ayan he has said the same thing to her, but she does not sound upset. Melek quite often did 'boy' things with boys, so perhaps this remark makes her less uncomfortable because she is confident that she is a girl and confident about border crossing. At the same time, she is sympathetic to Ayan, recognising that Jake's remark was intentionally insulting.

I tried several times to talk to the children about the girl and boy milk but could not get beyond common-sense replies. Ms Foster was aware of the boy/girl milk arguments but dealt with them by telling the children that all the milk comes from cows, and there is no difference in what is in the cartons. When I tried to ask the children more about the boy/girl milk legend, they ran a version of this adult answer past me, but this does not explain the intense emotions that were stirred by the gendered milk debates. I understand the milk saga as a ritual enactment of gender dichotomy and exploration of gender borders, which has deep emotional significance. I also wonder whether some of the boys found it disconcerting that both the cartons had pink logos and the milk came from female cows. They could not avoid associating themselves with femininity when they drank the milk.

Heterosexual games

Researchers have documented young children taking part in heterosexual girlfriend and boyfriend scenarios, enacting heterosexual practices of dumping, dating and 'going out', as well as episodes of kiss chase (Epstein, 1997; Connolly, 1998; Bhana, 2005; Renold, 2005). Boys and girls often played chasing games in the Reception playground at lunch times. Girls usually chased boys and captured and sometimes kissed them. In these chasing episodes girls seized moments of power through heterosexualised games. For short periods of time girls would work together to overwhelm individual boys and physically overpower them. Small groups of girls singled out a boy and chased him. When they caught him, the girls pulled him to the ground, pinned him down and kissed him. The encounters had a ritual quality of confrontation and oppositional gender positioning (Thorne, 1993; Bhana, 2005). I saw children new to Reception class watching these chasing games and taking part, as in the next episode:

> Two girls, Marsha and Lan, are chasing a boy, Jason.
>
> Lots of screaming and excitement.
>
> Marsha grabs Jason, gives him big kiss on cheek, runs off. He ostentatiously wipes off the kiss, runs after her.

Three girls, Shona, Molly and Lan chasing a boy, Kumi, down grass bank.

Shona and Lan push Kumi to the ground. Kiss him on his face. Kumi looks upset.

The girls who played these games seemed to find them very exciting, but the boys involved seemed more ambivalent. Researchers working with children aged 7 to 11 in primary schools have documented oppositional gender encounters where children explore and contest hegemonic gendered power relations (Thorne, 1993; Grugeon, 1993; Reay, 2001; Bhana, 2005; Renold, 2005). Thorne (1993) documents ritual episodes of cross-gender chasing, invasions and heterosexual teasing in USA elementary school playgrounds that evoke oppositional dualism and an exaggerated hegemonic view of gender difference. She observes that this oppositional play can also allow participants to exaggerate and even mock gender dichotomies and hegemonic power relations, and enable less powerfully positioned children to seize power, albeit briefly.

Grugeon (1993) documents many instances of English Primary girls' playground behaviour where they attempt to retaliate against boys' domination of physical space and resist boys' dominating presence through games, chants and rhymes that position boys as less powerful, or even ridiculous. She cites girls' rhymes where boys have pickles on their noses, boyfriends lose their underpants, and are threatened with having willies cut off. Bhana (2005) documents episodes in a South African playground where 7 and 8 year-old girls seize power for themselves by enacting a sexualised game, together lifting their dresses to show their panties, and taunting boys. These girls act out an aggressive sexuality in resistance to boys who mock, sexually harass and behave violently towards them. It is difficult for girls to position themselves in ways that do not reinforce hegemonic masculinity and these resistances are performed within a framework of heteronormativity.

Girls and occasionally boys played games that acted out heterosexual stories in their imaginative play scenarios. In small world play with a Magic Castle in Nursery, children often acted out scenes based on fairy tales where princesses were captured and princes rescued and kissed them. In Reception class, Molly and Nadia frequently put white veils on their heads and enacted heterosexualised scripts, such as weddings, in which they looked at themselves, danced in the mirror in the roleplay area, and talked about and acted out getting married to a prince. Sometimes girls acted out fairy stories such as Cinderella. Some were eager to tell me about their romances but also to make me aware that knew they were too young to have serious intentions.

Nadia to me (shyly, as if telling me a secret): 'Molly said I want to marry the Prince. We were only pretending though. We're not old enough.'

The girls were acting out heteronormative scripts in these roleplays. Comments made by staff suggested that they approved of such roleplays.

Mrs Jones: 'They look so cute! See how they wiggle those hips!'

Mrs Jones draws attention to the way that the girls embody heterosexualised gestures of emphasised femininity. Blaise (2005) documents numerous instances when young girls in a USA preschool embody and perform heterosexual femininities and I saw many instances in Ash Vale.

Butler emphasises the importance of embodiment, history, and lived experience, arguing that bodily acts as well as speech acts are performative, and can enable humans to rework and exceed gender norms. She insists that norms of recognition can change; they function to produce and to deproduce the notion of the human, and this opens up possibilities for transformation. She uses the term 'fantasy' to describe how we can explore embodied possibilities beyond norms and position ourselves 'otherwise'.

Fantasy is not the opposite of reality; it is what reality forecloses, and, as a result, it defines the limits of reality, constituting it as its constitutive outside. The critical promise of fantasy, when and where it exists, is to challenge the contingent limits of what will and will not be called reality. (Butler, 2004:29)

Butler's concept of fantasy fits with the ways in which the Ash Vale children acted out stereotypically heterosexual gender positions but in their roleplay also positioned themselves 'otherwise'.

Opportunities for developing new roleplay scenarios

The assortment of capes I introduced for imaginative play stimulated experimental and flexible approaches from the children over what they wore and the roles they took. Some of the boys developed hunting and rescue stories and some girls enacted superhero stories. In the following episode, Leonie takes on the role of Batman and encourages another girl, Madison, to join her. Leonie then takes up the character of Violet in the film *The Incredibles*. Although Violet does superhero deeds, it seems rather unfortunate that one of her major accomplishments is being able to disappear, as this tends to position girls as invisible rather than as active protagonists.

Leonie puts on gold shiny cape: 'I'm gonna wear this one. I'm gonna be Batman!'

(runs swiftly and lightly round the playground with arms outstretched 'Swish swish!' swooping and making 'Psh, psh' sounds to accompany her movements, absorbed in her performance).

Madison goes over to the capes, keeps touching the shiny pink one.

Leonie calls to Madison: 'You want to be Batman?'

Madison puts on a gold cape and follows Leonie round, copying her gestures.

Leonie: 'I gonna be Violet. Gonna disappear. Woosh!'

I encouraged the children to take on non gender-stereotyped roles but they often policed their own and one another's performances. Wearing capes did sometimes allow children to cross gender boundaries, as Ryan does below – although he is careful to make sure he is not observed by the others.

Ryan puts on a shiny pink cape and tiptoes round the play area. (He is on his own, so no chance of ridicule from other children).

Wearing a cape sometimes encouraged the wearer to make overtures to play with children they usually did not mix with. They seemed to feel freer to relate to each other in the capes, and I observed more eye contact between boys and girls, and more imitating of each other's actions, as in the following episode.

Leonie and Ben choosing capes. Both choose a white shiny cape.

Smile at each other, acknowledging they have the same outfit.

Leonie (arm outstretched): 'Pow! I can do magic!'

In the next play episode, Melek chooses a stereotypically feminine shiny pink cape and announces that she is a princess. But she behaves quite differently to the traditional fairy tale passive princess, positioning herself in a powerful role.

Melek puts on a pink shiny cape.

Melek:'I'm a princess' (runs around, making very fierce roaring noises and waving her arms, chasing Jake and Ryan, clearly having great fun).

In the following episode, I am reading the story about a girl called Rita, who becomes a superhero when she puts on special magic clothes (Offen, 1985). Two of the girls, Leonie and Tagan, are very interested, and Ho gets annoyed, saying that superheroes are 'for boys' and he pinches Leonie and tears the book. I had already spent a long time with Ho that morning, and I suspect he resented my attention going to the two girls.

Leonie and Tagan put on shiny capes, ask to read 'Rita the Rescuer' with me.

Leonie:'I can be a superhero.'

Leonie pointing to Rita:'She can be a superhero' (when Rita gets her magic clothes)

...

Leonie very enthusiastic and confident when she sees the pictures of the children who won't let Rita play. 'I can skip. I can play football.'

Tagan: 'Me too!'

(Our story is interrupted by Ho).

Ho comes over. He chooses a white shiny cape, the same as Leonie's.

Leonie (happily): 'I wearing a superhero cape. And I rescue the world.'

Ho: (loudly, pushing in front of Leonie): 'I'm the superhero it's for boys.'

Gets very annoyed when I am reading 'Rita' with Leonie and Tagan. He won't join us to listen to the story, tries to grab the book and tears a page. Pinches Leonie on her arm.

Leonie looks shocked and looks at me to see what I will do.

I tell Ho he is not to hurt Leonie or spoil the book and that he must go away if he will not share and listen. (I feel this is an inadequate response on my part. I should at least have got him to apologise to Leonie. At the time, I felt surprised and upset by his behaviour).

Ho goes away, I resume story with Leonie and Tagan.

...

After the story, Leonie puts on white cape, 'I like this cape!'

Leonie: 'She (Rita) was flying!' (very delighted).'I like to fly rescue everybody' (jumps around, arm outstretched) 'POW!'

Tagan copies her and they fly together.

With some support from me, Leonie and Tagan enjoyed experimenting with taking on superhero roles, but Ho's aggressive intervention shows how difficult it can be for girls to position themselves in ways that challenge dominant practices of masculinity. My response to his aggression did not, alas, support Leonie and Tagan adequately. Marsh's work with 6 and 7 year-olds (2000) shows how girls respond enthusiastically to opportunities to take part in superhero play as active protagonists when they have support.

Border crossing – daring to be different

Because there were so many instances of gender policing and separate play, my initial analysis of play episodes seemed to suggest separate cultures of boys and girls. However, as Thorne (1993) shows, if we ask the questions: how, when and where do girls and boys relate together? which girls, which boys relate together? we can begin to realise that separate cultures is only one, generally public, gender narrative. 'Daring to be different' is another. This encompasses children's desires and attempts to cross gender borders, and includes subversive struggles against school rules and assertions of aspects of identities being forged in home communities. It encompasses moments of collaboration and cooperation and fun between girls and boys that are not based on heterosexual teasing or flirtation. There is pleasure in knowing where you belong, and being acknowledged as a member of a community of shared ideas, outlooks and activities. There is also pleasure in taking control of new areas, exploring new ideas and forbidden territory. The unfamiliar or forbidden has an excitement of its own, although there is often a price to pay for daring to cross borders.

Newcomers in Nursery and Reception sometimes tried to engage in activities usually enacted by the opposite sex – but this was before they learned the rules from oldtimers. They soon learned that it was more acceptable to play with children of the same sex as themselves, at the appropriate masculine or feminine marked activities. In the following play sequence, Madison, one of the youngest girls in this Nursery group, tries to join in play with the garage and cars. Boys dominated play with the garage and girls rarely played with it. The boys' behaviour can be understood as policing the boundaries by preserving boy territory, although this is not made explicit. Madison is border crossing in the sense that she is trying to take part in an activity usually undertaken by boys, but she seemingly does not realise that, as a girl, this is not something she is expected to do. She told me she likes playing with cars at home.

Car mat and garage. Boys' domain. Lots of parallel play, lots of moving cars, and filling up with petrol, revving up and off. Reece, Ravi, Jake, joined by Harrison (comes from throwing big ball into net)

Femi joins.

Madison joins, picks up two cars, crashing them together, then runs round to (vacant) petrol pump on other side of table. Starts to fill up a truck very purposefully.

Jake takes Madison's truck from her

Madison: 'No, no, that's mine!'

Jake: 'No, I need it.' (Jake has made a line of vehicles in front of him, and adds Madison's truck to his line).

Madison starts to fill up another truck in the middle of the mat, and then adds this to Jake's line.

Jake moves in front of Madison and changes the dial on the petrol pump.

Madison reaches up and changes the dial again, looking at Jake.

Jake: 'No, no, (appealing to others) She's keeping that!

Jake, Ravi and Reece: 'Peep, pip, peep pip' (lots of loud aggressive noises).

Madison leaves the area, leaving five boys playing.

Here, the boys achieved dominance by making a lot of noise. They did not actually tell Madison to go away, but made it unpleasant for her to stay. She had not yet learned the rules for what the boys consider to be acceptable behaviour from girls. As a girl who wanted to play in a boy-dominated area, she lacked successful strategies for asserting herself in this situation, although she was initially quite assertive when Jake took a truck from her. Madison subsequently played mostly with dolls and buggies in the play-house, spending her time with younger girls, Madia and Nina. When she moved into Reception, she became rather withdrawn and I often saw her walking round with lunchtime supervisors at lunch play rather than playing with other children.

Three girls, Oni, Madison and Melek, seldom chose to go in the construction area in Reception class, although they often seemed to enjoy specific con-struction activities organised by the staff. Melek's behaviour was unusual for a girl in this setting: she often played chase, bean bags, skittles and imagina-tive games in the outdoor playground with some of the boys, Ryan, Jake, Daniel, Omar, Ben and Femi. Ms Kent was puzzled by Melek's behaviour:

Ms Kent: 'Melek is always playing with the boys. They seem to let her. Girls are usually more mumsy. Boys are more, um, I don't mean selfish, but they want their own time.'

Sitting on the bench in the playground at lunchtime, Melek had long con-versations with Ryan. She seemed to be comfortable playing with boys in her class and, as far as I know, was not teased or policed for this behaviour. In the following play episode, Melek seems to enjoy playing skittles with the boys, and she amuses Omar and Ryan when she puts a skittle cover on her head, pretending it is a new headscarf. Melek sometimes wore a headscarf to school, whereas Omar's mother always did, and here he and Melek share a moment of humour.

> Melek, Jake, Omar and Ryan chasing round skittles in *outdoor playground.*
>
> Daniel joins, picks up a skittle, chasing others, takes a skittle from Melek. All laughing.
>
> Melek (puts a skittle cover on her head): 'Ryan! Omar! Look at my new head-scarf!'
>
> Melek and Ryan run into the playhouse.
>
> Melek sits in the sink, swinging her legs and smiling.
>
> Ryan sits next to her.
>
> Omar puts the skittle cover on his head, laughing.
>
> Omar: 'Look Melek, this my Mum!'

Many of the boys seemed to enjoy playing imaginative games with Melek. Perhaps it is significant that Melek made no attempt to gain access to their specific masculine marked practices of hegemonic masculinity; construction, battle play or football and so did not threaten the boys' territory or expertise.

Some children in Ash Vale were able to cross gender boundaries successfully in imaginative play. One girl, Sara, was particularly adept. Right from her early days in Nursery she did so often in her imaginative play and she continued to border cross successfully as she got older. In the following play sequence we see Sara playing with the fire station. Sara has to work hard to maintain her position in the boys' play.

> *Fire station.* Boys domain.
>
> The only girl to play here all afternoon was Sara.
>
> 1.30 Sara joins fire station play with Daniel and Ryan.
>
> Daniel: 'Watch this Ryan!'
>
> Sara and Daniel lifting up firefighters, handling pieces quite roughly, engaging the firefighters in a kind of fight amongst themselves, with some attempts to make them use the hose and climb up the building, presumably to put out a fire. Lots of sounds, more like a battle than a rescue. Ryan parallel play on other side of table,

Daniel to Sara: 'Let me do that!' (grabbing firefighter from Sara, making lots of loud noises, 'rra, rrha' 'Inside!' (pushes the hose and firefighter into the building)

Sara: 'Eee!' (high squeal, as if surprised or alarmed, not clear if she in role here).

Daniel: 'I do that!'

Daniel (smashing his firefighter into Sara's firefighter): 'Ahra ra ra!' (roaring sound)

Sara to Daniel:'Look at the yellow ranger! Get off me'

Danie: 'Warrr warrr!'

Sara: 'Let me go!'

Daniel: 'Warr, war!' (continues loud noises, clashing firefighter onto Sara's area, looks triumphant, v amimated)

Sara: 'Let *me* go' (continues to advance her firefighter, does not seem distressed, fierce face, enjoying the 'battle'?).

Sara had to struggle to keep hold of some firefighters so she could join in the action with Daniel, but she managed to do so. It is perhaps significant that she chose this moment to sit at the fire station table, as there were only two boys and not five or six, as for most of the session. Six was the maximum allowed in the area, and there were only six chairs round the table.

What made it possible for Sara to border cross and play with something usually seen as a boys' game? Sara maintained and developed friendships with girls, but also took part in boys' activities, sometimes quietly, sometimes assertively. She was articulate and confident in a wide range of social situations in Nursery, spoke English and Farsi fluently, and she held her own in physical battle games.

Thorne's research with older primary age children in the USA (1993) shows that children who successfully border crossed were able to succeed because they wanted to engage in a particular activity and were prepared to persist in attempts to gain access to it in spite of the risk of being teased. Furthermore, Thorne found that having the skills and knowledge about the activity before they tried to join in increased their chances of acceptance. Sara border crossed successfully in Ash Vale Nursery because she was persistent and assertive, and she had the skills she needed to join in battle games.

Thorne (1993) points out that when children border cross successfully, they challenge oppositional gender relations. She suggests that this can only occur in interactions when gender-marking is minimal and heterosexual inter-pretations are avoided, and my research supports this view. Children border crossed in quiet moments, not through public displays, and they were usually the ones who were confident, even dominant within their same-sex friend-ship groups. Daniel was an articulate and popular boy who enjoyed close friendships with other boys and often took the lead in boys' games, but he also enjoyed border crossing. I often saw him playing quietly with dolls, parti-cularly bathing them in the water tray. He often finished his milk quickly and went outside to play at the water tray before the other boys came out.

Nursery Garden

Daniel on own at water tray, very carefully and gently bathing a doll, washing her hair and holding her.

Oni joins, parallel play.

Daniel leaves four minutes later when other boys come out.

Daniel told me that he enjoyed helping his Mum with his baby sister at home.

Implications for early childhood teaching and research

Staff in Ash Vale tried to encourage the children to take part in roleplay activities, but generally assumed that girls would want to take part in domestic roleplay and boys in superhero games. Yet imaginative play oppor-tunities and storytelling can enable young children to access alternative gender discourses and position themselves in powerful roles (Davies, 1989; Marsh, 2000).

There is a need for more research into gendered power relations in early years settings (Browne, 2004; MacNaughton, 2005). By exploring what gives children gender security and pleasure, we can appreciate the emotional investment they make in enacting particular practices of femininity and masculinity, and can gain insights into the difficulties children face when they cross gender boundaries. Although the children in my study usually policed roleplay clothes strictly, when I introduced an assortment of capes, they sometimes allowed each other to be more experimental and flexible in what they wore and the roles they took in imaginative play. Through opportunities like these, we can help children gain access to alternative discourses that enable them to gain pleasure and empowerment beyond gender dualism.

Staff contributed to the naturalisation of battle games by variously condoning the battles, forbidding excessively boisterous and potentially violent aspects, and expecting boys to want to take part because they were naturally keen on superhero play. As Holland (2003) argues, a ban on weapon play in early years settings and constant negative feedback about fighting games causes boys to engage in such behaviour covertly and prevents any discussion or development of play themes. Marsh (2000) and Holland (2003) suggest that children be encouraged to extend their play through imaginative themes such as rescues, and the exploration of good and evil.

Checklist for action for gender equity

- Monitor socio-dramatic and imaginative play in your early years settings. Observe who takes on which roles and who dominates play. Are some children excluded? Who takes control and how do they do so? Discuss play themes with colleagues and with the children. What kinds of play are pleasurable and why?

- Provide an assortment of non-gendered props and items for dressing up. Assorted pieces of cloth can be bought cheaply and have multiple uses in imaginative play.

- Make opportunities for staff to play with children in roleplay areas and spend time there yourself so you can help children develop socio-dramatic play and imaginative play beyond gendered stereotypes.

- Introduce new stories and roleplay situations to encourage children to experiment with positioning themselves in new ways, by acting out characters and creating their own storylines. Support children who resist gender stereotyped play by playing alongside them in the roleplay areas and help children make their own imaginative story books by scribing for them.

- Understand why boys enjoy battle and superhero play. Do not allow superhero play to dominate all areas of the classroom or playground. Support children who dislike battle play. Encourage children to develop positive imaginative superhero play through stories and drama.

- Do not reinforce gender dualism by suggesting that girls' domestic play is good and boys' superhero play is bad. Do not assume that all girls will want to play in domestic roleplay areas or that all boys will want to take part in superhero play.

6
Where do we go from here?

Fantasy is what allows us to imagine ourselves and others otherwise, it esta-
blishes the possible in excess of the real; it points elsewhere, and when it is
embodied, it brings the elsewhere home. (Butler, 2004: 29)

This chapter summarises key points from my research in Ash Vale and
the implications for early years education and gender equity. I suggest
how early years educators and researchers can work with young children to find out about their understandings of gender. If we understand how
and why children learn to see themselves as boys or as girls we can find ways
to help them make play choices beyond gender stereotypes.

Masculinities and femininities in Ash Vale
My research shows how newcomers to the early years classes learned from
established children that some play activities were for girls and others were
for boys. New children had first to establish themselves as legitimate peripheral participants in gendered play and, as their skills and knowledge increased, they were gradually allowed to take a fuller part in the communities
of practice.

Young boys in Ash Vale learned from the older boys that they needed to adopt
play practices of hegemonic masculinity in order to claim legitimacy as a
participant in communities of masculinity. The practices of hegemonic masculinity were football, construction activities, battle games and associated
superhero play, and the boys who took part in them were able to gain access
to space, resources and comradeship with other boys. To become a full
member of the communities of practice of masculinity in the early years
classes, boys had to demonstrate knowledge and skills in these play practices.
They learned to exclude girls, and younger and weaker boys. Masculinity had

to be earned and repeatedly demonstrated. Boys had a good deal of emotional investment in battle play, and they learned to embody this practice of hege-monic masculinity as a key way of demonstrating membership of the com-munity of practice of masculinity in school.

Teachers and support staff discouraged rough physical play and violent play themes. Their disapproval of a central practice of hegemonic masculinity had a serious impact on the children and reinforced gender dualism. Some boys experienced extra pleasure from evading adults' gaze when they played battle games (Foucault, 1976). The violent reaction of Ho (p133) when Leonie and Tagan positioned themselves as superheroes was unusual, but it demon-strates the force some boys will employ if their hegemony is threatened. Ho's reaction may have been especially vehement because, as a new boy, he was still trying to gain acceptance into the community of practice of Reception boys.

Girls learned to embody femininities through domestic and fairy tale role-plays, skipping games, fashion and adoption of pink in their clothing and accessories. They learned to monitor their appearances and embody 'sensible good girl'. The staff showed approval for girls' domestic play themes centred on families and fairy tales, and girls gained pleasure from positioning them-selves in ways that earned them adult approval. Some girls positioned them-selves as virtuous by condemning boys' violent games and reporting them, thus making a virtue of necessity as the boys did not allow them to participate in these games. That no teachers or support staff were male added to the polarisation of male and female spheres.

Children in Ash Vale were subject to panoptic surveillance, which encouraged them to monitor their own behaviour. Not only did they position themselves as good school pupil, but they also performed oppositional masculinities and femininities. Girls took up 'sensible' and 'helpful' positions in school, in con-trast to boys' enactment of 'silly' and 'selfish' positions (Francis, 1998, 2000). The public nature of many gender performances, on the carpet and in the playground, contributed to mutual panoptic surveillance, as children were quick to notice and comment on any deviation from the norms.

Young children have little personal history or life experience to draw on in positioning themselves, and are constantly using their imagination and infor-mation from their senses to trying to modify and extend their understanding of how they should act. They are quick to pick up on clues given by other chil-dren and adults about what behaviour is valued and what will earn them recognition and praise. Davies (1989) demonstrates how young children often behave quite differently in different social situations. In Ash Vale I observed a huge contrast between behaviour in the playground, where children enacted practices from childhood cultures, and on the carpet in class, where they enacted practices of schooling, as pupils. Conflicts in positioning arise for young children who want to run, move freely and expansively, but want also to please teachers and carers who encourage them to restrain their physical movement.

Children also experienced emotional and cognitive dilemmas when objects of knowledge required conflicting subject positions. So, for example, some young girls wanted to position themselves as correctly feminine, by wearing girlie pink dressing up items, but also wanted to experience pleasure and power by wearing masculine marked items such as fire-fighters' and foot-ballers' costumes. Young boys wanted to position themselves as correctly masculine, by taking part in activities such as superhero play and battle games but some wanted also to experience pleasure in feminine marked activities such as domestic play. Thus the children were often positioned within conflicting discourses. Individual gender identities are forged in the resolution of such conflict. Discourses of fair play and equality clashed with discourses of security and traditional gender roles. Desire for adventure conflicted with desires to be accepted and avoid teasing and ridicule.

My research shows that successful border crossing was possible when the child was already a confident established member of the appropriate community of practice. Those who have learned the rules and taught them to others are better able to resist and rework aspects of hegemonic gender discourses. Sara, Melik and Daniel were particularly successful in positioning themselves 'otherwise' by border crossing.

Relationships and power relations between the children were complex and shifted in time and space. The children participated in play practices that reproduced dualistic femininities and masculinities and they policed each other's behaviour and also their own. I saw Fifi playing with footballs in the Nursery garden at first, but as her efforts were opposed and she was marginalised by older boys, she increasingly went to play with girls, pushing dolls in prams. This is surely not a free choice on her part. It demonstrates how girls' femininities are deeply embedded in heteronormativity. Staff praised Fifi for behaviour that prefigures her expected future role as mother and carer.

It was similarly difficult for young boys to resist the practices of hegemonic masculinity, and their behaviour was policed by other children and sometimes adults when they did anything that was associated with femininity, such as when Omar tried to be an angel or imagined himself playing with a Barbie. Transgressing gender norms can incur a high penalty. As Blaise's research in a USA preschool shows (2005), the support of a member of staff or other adult is often crucial to young children enjoying subverting gender norms.

Teachers in Ash Vale were obliged to deliver a Literacy programme that emphasised rote teaching of phonics, often decontextualised and not related to literature, so felt they had no time to help the children develop creative writing and dramatic play themes. I believe this had a detrimental effect on the development of children's identities. As Marsh points out (2005), children's identity development is linked with acquisition of skills, knowledge and understanding in communication, language and literacy.

> As well as recognising and valuing children's cultural experiences, teachers need also to give permission for children to reflect on ways in which their subjectivities have been shaped by the literacy experiences encountered in school and in out-of-school settings. (Marsh, 2005)

Helping young children play beyond gender stereotypes

It can be difficult for early years staff to seize moments when they can usefully intervene in gendered play, because play episodes are often short and because discourses and practices based on gender dualism are so entrenched that they go unnoticed. It is also difficult to intervene to support a child who is trying to border cross. So, for example, we saw how Mrs Teal tried to tell Daniel that 'girls can be footballers' but this was not sufficient to support Tia in her choice to position herself as a footballer. While Mrs Teal was talking to Daniel, Tia gave up her attempts to wear a football tabard and the moment was lost. Looking at this play episode again reveals other ways Mrs Teal could have supported Tia.

> Daniel (indicating Tia): 'She's taking off her coat.'
>
> Mrs Teal: 'That's ok because she's putting on a tabard.'
>
> Daniel: 'No, but that's for boys. Boys are footballers.'
>
> Mrs Teal: 'She can be a lady footballer. There are ladies' football teams as well as men's teams.'
>
> Daniel: 'No, it's men's football. Ladies don't play real football.'
>
> Tia quietly takes off the football tabard and starts a cheerleader dance with the pompoms instead.

Daniel goes on to talk about football games he has seen on TV and names famous male footballers.

Perhaps Mrs Teal could have put up posters or photos of women playing football beside the football tabards, and encouraged Tia and her friends to start a girls' football team. This would also have provoked discussion about football and gender positions.

Remember that Daniel too wanted to cross gender borders when he hurried to finish his milk and go out to bathe the dolls in the water tray (see p121). Daniel also needed support to cross gender borders in his play but would not have wanted adults to draw other boys' attention to his desire to play with dolls. In situations like this, roleplay and drama give children safe spaces to try out alternative gender positions. A roleplay area could be set up as, for example, a baby clinic or crèche.

The play resources provided affected how children relate together. The younger, less skilled children all played with balls when plenty were supplied, but were excluded by the dominant boys when only a few were available. The lunch playtime in Ash Vale was a key site for the production of gendered identities and children were pressed to conform to oppositional gender norms. Lunch time can be up to a sixth of the time children spend in school each day so it is important to study how and what children are learning during this time.

Adults and older children are important role models for younger children in early years settings. Encouragement to experiment with non-stereotyped gender roles enables them to experiment with a range of positions. Contemporary mass media and toy advertising skews children's play options because toys and games are heavily marketed at either girls or boys. A limited range of toys – predominantly pink and centred on domestic play, crafts and Barbies – are marketed for girls, while weapons, superhero and construction toys, and nearly everything requiring active play are marketed for boys. But gendered play options can be challenged within early years classrooms by adding specific play items to the dressing up and roleplay clothes and props, art and craft materials for construction.

Storybooks can challenge gender stereotyped thinking. Early years educators need to allocate time to play with children in the roleplay areas and discuss gender and equity issues in ways that help develop critical thinking and explore narratives that challenge dualistic gender positions. Adult support is particularly important in superhero play.

Superhero play

Superhero discourses that circulate through films, computer games, TV and media images impact on how boys enact superhero scripts. The media and toy industries manipulate boys' interest and some reflect sexist and racist stereotypes (Marsh, 2000). The principle discourse of masculinity available to boys in commercial superhero stories is 'tough', violent and heterosexual (Browne, 2004). As she argues, many boys enjoy superhero play and physical play embodying physical strength and domination because it signifies male power. They explore ways of enacting masculinities by competitive, combative displays of power. Davies (1989) showed how boys' superhero play often positions them as heroic, and my findings confirm this. We need to acknowledge the attraction popular culture holds for children, whilst encouraging them to question its negative stereotypes.

'Playfighting' rarely leads to real fights, although, as Holland (2003) points out, it is important that educators help children to resist 'playfighting' behaviour if children say they dislike or are upset by it. Rich (2003) shows how adults can provide role models, vocabulary and resources for children to develop fantasy play, and encourage collaboration and exploration of issues of concern such as war and violence. The Ash Vale children's use of capes suggest that young boys and girls are keen to explore new story lines, if they have suitable encouragement and props, but also that boys have emotional investment in enacting battle scenes and that they learn to embody this practice of hegemonic masculinity as a key way of demonstrating membership of the community of practice of masculinity in school.

Young girls often do not want to engage in superhero play (Browne, 2004) and when they do, their play centres on female heroism that is defined by qualities of endurance and kindness, in contrast to boys' scripts that involve physical strength and use of violence. Marsh (2000) found that when presented with active female heroes, 6 and 7-year old girls were interested in superhero play. Certainly, the girls in my study were keen to read and make up stories about female superheroes.

Some girls drew on images from a film that was popular at the time of my fieldwork, *The Incredibles*. Two female characters have powerful central roles, although the script is heteronormative, and they are portrayed as less strong than the male characters. This emphasises the need for young children to have access to alternative stories that include a range of sexualities and gender positions. As Marsh argues, 'In order for girls to take a more active part in heroic discourses, teachers need to ensure that they create the conditions in which this can happen. Girls need to feel safe and be given permission and space in which to explore these roles' (Marsh, 2000:219).

Young children make emotional investments when they take up masculine and feminine positions in play and need to be encouraged to experiment with a range of gender roles. If we explore what gives children gender security and pleasure, we can gain insights into the difficulties they face when they cross gender boundaries. Imaginative play opportunities and storytelling can help them access alternative gender positions and position themselves in powerful roles (Davies, 1989; Marsh, 2000).

Implications for early years education and research

The enduring reliance on principles of DAP is probably the greatest impediment to gender equity work. I often heard teachers, teaching assistants and meals supervisors maintaining that differences between boys and girls are natural and innate and that access to greater equal opportunities would therefore not change their behaviour significantly. If, however, staff monitor the play practices in their setting, paying particular attention to power relationships, observing how the children learn from each other and how children gain pleasure and satisfaction, they might discover that this is not the case. They might see that they unwittingly reinforce gender dualism. Alternative play scenes can be set up that support children in their experiments with gender positions by discussing their choices and beliefs. Early years educators need focused inservice education to consider how beliefs learned in initial teacher training prevent much-needed interventions to help children gain access to a wide range of play options (MacNaughton, 2000).

Young children learn that if they want to be a successful member of an early years class they must behave in ways that show they are a girl or a boy. It is therefore crucial for early years teachers to focus on issues of gender equity at all stages of their curriculum planning and delivery. Young children need opportunities to talk about and experiment with a range of gender positions. Children can be flexible and adaptable if they receive encouragement and permission to experiment. Researchers can actively promote gender equity by working with young children to explore their understandings of gender.

Attention must be paid to the power relations between children within early years settings. Children's play choices and styles should be observed in specific settings, to see which children dominate activities in various spaces and at different times, who takes control and how they achieve domination. Settings can vary, and things can change in a short time – as the new children become the oldtimers. Early years educators need to talk with the children and discuss gender issues to find out how they experience their settings.

Opportunities to work collaboratively and cooperatively in a variety of same-sex and mixed groups can strengthen young children's ability to position themselves in new ways. Early years educators need to intervene in play practices to ensure that all children have access to a wide range of play equipment, by introducing strategies such as timed periods of play, and periods of access for girls only or boys only.

When children cross gender borders, early years educators need to recognise what they are doing and that it is difficult for them to do it, and be prepared to talk with the children who attempt to police them. Children who are engaging in non-stereotypically gendered behaviours also need support. Successful border crossing might be fleeting and can, as we saw, easily be missed in a busy classroom or playground.

Early years educators and researchers need to focus on the relational aspects of young children's identity development and observe how they develop gender identities in relation to identities of ethnicity, class, sexuality, age and (dis)ability. Children's play practices and schooling practices often encourage gender differences and heteronormativity, and thereby contribute to inequity. Initial training and continuous professional development programmes are needed, to help staff think and act to promote equity in early years settings.

Suggestions for further research

There is a view that children are too young to consider issues of social justice, but this is not so. My research findings support studies that show children are aware of, and participate in, discourses of power relations, normalisation and social and cultural differences from a very young age (Robinson and Jones Diaz, 2006:143). These authors show how diversity and difference are often located in a discourse of deficit, a discourse which was evident at Ash Vale where it operated through normalising schooling practices in relation to dominant constructions of ethnicity, class and bilingualism. The staff drew on discourses of childhood that emphasise a homogenous so-called 'universal' experience of being a child, and of child development theories that do not allow for the complexities and contradictions of children's experiences of multiple identities across different social and cultural contexts.

Further research is needed to examine how children are positioned within the discourses and regulatory practices they encounter, and how they position themselves, as active participants and learners within discourses of gender, race, class, (dis)ability and sexuality. As Robinson and Jones Diaz (2006) argue, children's choices are located in relation to neo-liberal frameworks and discourses of individualism but children are, at the same time, active agents in the construction of their own identity: they are able to act with intent.

My findings support research by Browne (2004), MacNaughton (2005) and Thorne (1993). We show that there are possibilities for reworking gender positions within discourses through borderwork. It is at the margins – at the borders – that possibilities exist to 'work the weakness in the norm' (Butler, 2004). It is possible to imagine and realise the potential of fantasy beyond heteronormativity and gender dualism by thinking, speaking and acting 'otherwise'. Resisting norms often results in punishment, but not resisting can be 'the social death of a person' (Butler, 2004).

Further research could usefully explore how young children's imaginative play constructs and embodies a range of femininities and masculinities. By experimenting with different gender positions, young children can take risks in relative safety, and try out alternative ways of doing boy and girl. Small scale action research projects which monitor play in early years settings and provide opportunities for children to try out a range of activities without fear of ridicule will empower children to make bold play choices. Children can be actively involved in developing transgressive gender constructs and challenging gender dualism. Children in Ash Vale showed that they could indeed take up different gender positions, when the situation and the relations of power permitted. As Butler (2004) observed, children have keen imaginative powers, and can, with support, think and act 'otherwise'.

Working for gender equity
Key points emerged from research in Ash Vale:
- Young children learn how to do boy or girl in early years classes by observing older children and gradually taking a fuller part in play activities with other children.
- Power relations between children are key to understanding why boys and girls play in same-sex groups and at different activities. In Ash Vale early years classes boys took power and dominated space through football, battle games and construction, while girls seized power through roleplay and skipping. Girls used 'pink' as a symbol of femininity, and boys saw 'pink' as a pollutant.
- Young children often limit their play choices because they need to show other children that they understand the correct behaviour for

girls and for boys. They learn that certain ways of behaving will gain them pleasure and recognition, whilst others will bring them hostility and ridicule.

■ Despite the stated wishes of early years educators to develop gender equity, schooling practices often emphasise stereotypical differences between boys and girls and foster differentials in power.

■ Even when early educators attempt to show children that boys and girls have free choice in play activities, what children experiences in early years classes tells them a different story.

■ It is difficult for young children to cross gender boundaries in their play because other children police play activities so strictly. To cross gender borders, children generally need adult support to succeed.

Promoting gender equity in early years settings: A checklist for action

■ Observe the kinds of play that take place in your early years setting throughout the day. Who plays what, when? Who is included? Who is excluded? Who takes power, where and when?

■ Monitor who uses different spaces within the classrooms and play-grounds

■ Monitor how adults talk to children in the setting, for example, do they reinforce gender difference by saying 'you boys ... you girls'? What do they praise girls and boys for?

■ Talk to the children about their play choices and encourage them to ask questions about girls' and boys' activities and gender roles

■ Take time to play with children in roleplay areas and extend the range of possibilities by modelling non-stereotypical and alternative gender roles

■ Encourage children to try new activities and take on different roles in imaginative play

■ Provide non-gender marked dressing-up clothes so that young children have opportunities to try out alternative gender positions in safety

■ Actively support children who try to cross gender boundaries in their play, e.g introduce timed sessions for girls only construction play and football

■ Intervene if superhero or football play is taking over all the play space

■ Remember that young children have an emotional investment in getting their gendered behaviour correct and do not be discouraged if you feel your efforts are making little difference. You *are* making a difference to children's life chances by presenting them with alternative ways of doing gender and by encouraging them to question gender stereotypes

Glossary

community of practice – a group engaging in a shared practice.

Children learn what it is to be masculine or feminine through legitimate peripheral participation in communities of femininity and masculinity of older children and adults. At the same time, children are full participants in communities of practice of girls and boys of a similar age to themselves. Boys can been seen as apprentice men, and girls as apprentice women, learning through observation and peripheral participation what it means to be a man or a woman in the local communities of practice in which they live. The naming of a baby as a boy or girl places the child within a particular community of practice, and this performative naming results in differential treatment and expectations (Paechter, 2007).

compulsory heterosexuality – discourses that presume females and males are inevitably sexually attracted to each other.

developmentally appropriate practice (DAP) – education that provides appropriate stimulating play experiences to enable individual children to progress through defined developmental stages. Emphasises child-centred active learning, free experimentation and discovery.

discourse – social, institutional and emotional frameworks and practices through which humans make meanings of their experiences. A discourse refers to a way of speaking, writing, interacting or thinking that is made up of particular given truths that define what can and cannot be included, said or done (Paechter, 1998).

embodiment – the social process of bodily inscription.
As human beings, we become embodied in discourses, through conscious and unconscious thoughts, emotions and bodily performances (Weedon, 1987). Who we are is intimately bound up with what we do, in the sense that our thoughts, desires, feelings and bodies are developed in relation to each other. We embody our experiences. So, for example a person who becomes a singer or carpenter or athlete comes to embody certain associated characteristics such as determination,

patience, sense of rhythm, manual dexterity, strong muscles. What we can embody depends on factors such as our age and physical strength and these are linked to social and cultural factors. We take on multiple roles and we embody many different attributes at any one time, which can change as we live our lives. So for example being a mother or father can be uppermost at one stage of life.

emphasised femininity – discourses that position women/girls in ways that re-inforce male power and emphasise compliance, nurture and empathy (Connell, 1987, 2002).

ethnicity – a group of people who share certain aspects of culture, such as religion, language, and customs.

feminist poststructuralist – Relationships between individuals and social institutions are seen to be inseparable and interdependent, and power is seen as a central dynamic in relationships. Gender is socially constructed in discourse (Weedon 1999).

gender – the ways that children are positioned as male or female within power and knowledge relations.

gender borderwork – interactions between girls and boys, whether used to police gender boundaries and keep girls and boys separate, or when children cross gender boundaries, or when girls and boys explore activities and relationships with each other.

Some children attempt to position themselves in ways that challenge stereotypical behaviour. Sometimes they do so successfully by embodying what appears to be a contradiction, for example, a girl who plays football, or makes model cars, in a culture where these activities are designated as only for boys.

gender dualism – ideas which suggest that boys and girls are naturally different.

hegemony – social ascendancy of certain groups that is achieved not through brute force or violence but through cultural processes and institutions.

hegemonic masculinity – discourses of dominant masculinity that position some boys/men and women/girls as subordinate or inferior (Connell, 1987).

identity – ways we construct meanings about ourselves.
Identity development is an active process that continues throughout our lives as we engage with people. Our identities are not fixed but are negotiated and developed over a lifetime, and they are fluid, multiple and relational. The range of subject positions available to us depends on the social relations of power operating within particular situations and discourses of difference, including gender, age, ethnicity, sexuality, class and ability (Weedon, 1987).

heteronormative – discourses that position heterosexual relationships as natural, positioning other sexual relationships as inferior or deviant.

heteronormativity – construction of gender and desire by which heterosexuality is positioned as the norm, against which other sexual relationships are constructed as Other, inferior, deviant (Epstein and Johnson, 1994; Paechter, 1998; Kehily, 2001).

legitimate peripheral participation – new members of a group are permitted to take part in minor aspects of a central activity (Lave and Wenger, 1991).

masculinities and femininities – ways in which we perform as a boy or girl, man or woman, throughout our lifetime, by demonstrating through actions, thoughts, speech, and bodily gestures our understanding of ourselves as male or female. Masculinity and femininity are often constructed in a dualistic relationship to each other, positioning femininity as a lack, an absence of masculinity (Paechter, 2006).

Other – to be positioned as an outsider, an 'out' group as opposed to an 'in' group. The Subject is defined through exclusion of the Other. Other is positioned as inferior eg man as Subject, woman as Other (Paechter, 1998).

panoptic surveillance – group members exert a disciplinary gaze on one another and on themselves. This encourages conformity to the norms of the group.

play technologies – ways children applied knowledge and skills to particular uses of play objects such as skipping ropes and footballs.

'race' – a group of people who may share some physical characteristic to which social importance is attached.

racism – belief that one 'race' is superior to others, coupled with power to put this belief into practice (Gaine and George, 1999).

reification – the process by which certain objects and practices are taken as markers of community membership or points of focus for organising the negotiation of meanings within communities of practice (Wenger, 1998).

sex – children's assigned gender label of boy or girl.

Key to transcripts

...	material edited out
(comment)	background information, information re gestures, movements
???	inaudible responses
italic	emphasis given by speaker

Symbols adapted from Renold, 2005

References

Alldred, P (1998) Ethnography and discourse analysis: dilemmas in representing the voices of children. In J.Ribbens and R.Edwards (eds) *Feminist Dilemmas in Qualitative Research*. London: Sage Publications

Archer, L (2003) *Race, masculinity and schooling: Muslim boys and education*. Maidenhead: Open University Press

Aubrey, C, David, T, Godfrey, R, Thompson, L (2000) *Early Childhood Educational Research: Issues in methodology and ethics*. London: RoutlegeFalmer

Ball, S.J (1990) Self-doubt and soft data: social and technical trajectories in ethnographic fieldwork. *Qualitative Studies in Education* 3 (2) p157-171

Barth, F (1969) *Ethnic Groups and Boundaries: The Social Organization of Cultural Differences*. Little, Brown and Co.

Baxter, J (2003) *Positioning Gender in Discourse: A Feminist Methodology*. New York: Palgrave MacMillan

Best, R (1983) *We've All Got Scars: What Girls and Boys Learn in Elementary School*. Bloomington: Indiana University Press

Bhana, D (2005) 'Show me the panties': girls play games in the school playground. In C.Mitchell and J.Reid-Walsh (eds) *Seven Going on Seventeen*. New York, NY: Peter Lang

Blaise, M (2005) *Playing it Straight*. London: Routledge

Bordo, S (2004) *Unbearable Weight: Feminism, Western Culture and the Body*. California: University of California Press

Bredekamp, S (1987) *Developmentally Appropriate Practice in Early Childhood Programmes serving Children from Birth through Age 8*. National Association for the Education of Young Children: Washington DC

British Educational Research Association (2004) *Revised Ethical Guidelines for Educational Research*. BERA

Brown, B (1998) *Unlearning Discrimination in the Early Years*. Stoke on Trent: Trentham Books

Browne, N (2004) *Gender Equity in the Early Years*. Maidenhead: Open University Press

Bruner, J (1986) *Actual Minds, Possible Worlds*. Harvard: Harvard University Press

Buchbinder, D (1994) *Masculinities and Identities*. Melbourne: Melbourne University Press

Burman, E (1994) *Deconstructing Developmental Psychology*. London: Routledge

Butler, J (1990) *Gender Trouble: feminism and the subversion of identity*. London: Routledge

Butler, J (1993) *Bodies that matter: on the discursive limits of 'sex'*. London: Routledge

Butler, J (2004) *Undoing Gender*. New York, NY: Routledge

Cannella, G.S (1997) *Deconstructing Early Childhood Education: Social Justice and Revolution.* New York: Peter Lang Publishing

Carlspecken, P.F (1996) *Critical Ethnography in Educational Research.* New York, NY: Routledge

Connell, R.W (1987) *Gender and Power.* Cambridge: Polity Press

Connell, R.W (1995) *Masculinities.* Cambridge: Polity Press

Connell, R.W (2002) *Gender.* Cambridge, Polity Press

Connolly, P (1998) *Racism, Gender Identities and Young Children.* London: Routledge

Connolly, P (2003) Gendered and gendering spaces: playgrounds in the early years. In C.Skelton and B.Francis (eds) *Boys and girls in the Primary Classroom.* Maidenhead: Open University Press

Connolly, P (2004) *Boys and Schooling in the Early Years.* London: RoutledgeFalmer

Corsaro, W.A (1981) Entering the child's world – research strategies for field entry and data collection in a preschool setting. In J.L.Green and C.Wallat (eds) *Ethnography and Language in Education Settings.* Norwood, NJ: Ablex Publishing

Christensen, P and James, A (eds) (2000) *Research with Children: perspectives and practices.* London: Falmer Press

Davies, B (1989) *Frogs and Snails and Feminist Tales.* London: Allen and Unwin

Davies, B (1998) The politics of category membership in early childhood settings. In N.Yelland (ed) *Gender in Early Childhood.* London: Routledge

Donaldson, M (1978) *Children's Minds.* London: Fontana

Douglas, M (1966) *Purity and Danger.* London: Routledge Classics

Dunn, J (1998) Young children's understanding of other people: evidence from within the family. In M.Woodhead, D. Faulkner, K. Littleton (eds) *Cultural Worlds of Childhood.* London: Routledge

Epstein, D (1997) Cultures of Schooling/Cultures of Sexuality, *International Journal of Inclusive Education,* 1, 37-53.

Epstein, D (1998) Are you a girl or are you a teacher? In G.Walford (ed) *Doing Research about Education.* London: Falmer Press

Epstein, D (1999) Sex Play: romantic significations, sexism and silences in the schoolyard. In D.Epstein and J.T.Sears. *A Dangerous Knowing: sexuality, pedagogy and popular culture.* London: Cassell

Epstein, D and Johnson, R (1994) On the straight and narrow: the heterosexual presumption, homophobias and schools. In D. Epstein (ed.) *Challenging Lesbian and Gay Inequalities in Education.* Buckingham: Open University Press

Farrell, A (2005) *Ethical Research with Children.* Oxford: Oxford University Press

Foucault, M (1976) *The History of Sexuality Vol.1: An Introduction.* London: Penguin

Foucault, M (1977) *Discipline and Punish.* London: Penguin

Foucault, M (1978) *The History of Sexuality Volume 1.* New York: Vintage Books

Foucault, M (1980) *Power/Knowledge: Selected Interviews and Other Writings 1972-1977.* London: Harvester Press

Francis, B (1998) *Power Plays.* Stoke on Trent: Trentham Books

Francis, B (2000) *Boys, Girls and Achievement: Addressing the Classroom Issues.* London: RoutledgeFalmer

Frye, M (1983) *The Politics of Reality: Essays in Feminist Theory.* New York, NY: The Crossing Press

Gagen, E (2000) Playing the part: performing gender in America's playgrounds. In S. Holloway and G. Valentine (eds) *Children's Geographies: Playing, living and learning.* London, Routledge

Gaine, C and George, R (1999) *Gender, 'Race' and Class in Schooling.* London: Falmer

Garvey, C (1990) *Play.* Cambridge, Mass: Harvard University Press

George, R (2007) *Girls in a Goldfish Bowl.* Rotterdam, Netherlands: Sense Publishers

Gilroy, P (1993) *Small Acts.* London: Serpents Tail

Gordon, T and Lahelma, E (1996) 'School is Like an Ant's Nest': spatiality and embodiment in schools. *Gender and Education* 8(3) p301-310

Gramsci, A (1971) *Selections from the Prison Notebooks.* London: Lawrence and Wishart

Grant, V (2002) Understanding gender issues in preschool settings. In C.Nutbrown (ed) *Research Studies in Early Childhood Education.* Stoke on Trent: Trentham

Grieshaber, S and Cannella, G.S (eds) (2001) *Embracing Identities in Early Childhood Education: Diversity and Possibilities.* New York: Teachers College Press

Grugeon, E (1993) Gender implications of children's playground culture. In P.Woods and M. Hammersley (eds) *Gender and Ethnicity in Schools.* Routledge, London

Hall, S (1980) Race, articulation and societies structured in dominance. In *UNESCO, Sociological Theories: Race and Colonialism.* Paris: UNESCO

Hall, S (1992) New ethnicities. In J.Donald and A.Rattansi (eds) *Race, Culture and Difference.* London: Sage

Hall, S (1996) Introduction: Who needs 'identity?' In S.Hall and P. du Gay (eds) *Questions of Cultural Identity.* London: Sage

Hatcher, R (1995) Racism and children's cultures. In M.Griffiths and B. Troyna (eds) *Antiracism, Culture and Social Justice in Education.* Stoke on Trent: Trentham Books

Holland, P (2003) *We Don't Play With Guns Here: war, weapon and superhero play in the early years.* Buckingham: Open University Press

Ivinson, G and Murphy, P (2007) *Rethinking Single-Sex Teaching.* Oxford: Oxford University Press

James, A and Prout, A (eds) (1997) *Constructing and Reconstructing Childhood: Contemporary issues in the Sociological Study of Childhood.* London: Falmer Press

Jenks, C (1996) *Childhood.* London: Routledge

Jordan, E (1995) Fighting boys and fantasy play: the construction of masculinity in the early years of school, *Gender and Education* 7(1) p69-86

Kehily, M (2001) Issues of gender and sexuality in schools. In B. Francis and C.Skelton (eds) *Investigating Gender.* Buckingham: Open University Press

Kehily, M.J (ed) (2004) *An Introduction to Childhood Studies.* Oxford: Oxford University Press

Lather, P (1991) *Getting Smart: Feminist Research and Pedagogy With/in the Postmodern.* Routledge, Chapman and Hall, Inc.

Lave, J and Wenger, E (1991) *Situated Learning: Legitimate peripheral participation.* Cambridge: Cambridge University Press

Lewis, A (1992) Group child interviews as a research tool, *British Educational Research Journal* 18(4) p413-21

Lloyd, B and Duveen, G (1992) *Gender Identities and Education: The impact of starting school.* Hemel Hempstead: Harvester Press

MacNaughton, G (1998) Improving our gender equity 'tools': a case for discourse analysis. In N.Yelland (ed) *Gender in Early Childhood.* London: Routledge

MacNaughton, G (2000) *Rethinking Gender in Early Childhood Education.* London: Sage Publications

MacNaughton, G (2005) *Doing Foucault in Early Childhood Studies.* London: Routledge

Marsh, J (2000) 'But I want to fly too!': girls and superhero play in the infant classroom, *Gender and Education* 12(2) p209-220

Marsh, J (2005) Ritual, performance and identity construction. In J. Marsh (ed) *Popular culture, new media and digital literacy in early childhood.* London: RoutledgeFalmer

Martin, B (2010) 'You've got to have the pink one because you're a girl!': exploring young girls' understanding of femininities and masculinities in preschool. In C.Jackson, C.Paechter and E.Renold (eds) *Girls and Education 3-16 Continuing Concerns, New Agendas.* Maidenhead: Open University Press

Mayall, B (2002) *Towards a Sociology of Childhood.* Oxford: Oxford University Press

Miles, M (1983) *Racism.* London: Routledge

Mirza, H.S (1992) *Young, Female and Black.* London: Routledge

Moss, P and Penn, H (1996) *Transforming Nursery Education.* London: Paul Chapman

Narayan, U (1989) The project of feminist epistemology: perspectives from non-western feminists. In A.M. Jagger and S.R.Bordo (eds) *Gender/Body/Knowledge: Feminist Reconstructions of Being and Knowing.* New Brunswick NJ: Rutgers University Press

Nespor, J (1997) *Tangled up in School.* Mahwah, New Jersey: Lawrence Erlbaum Associates

Ofsted (2007) *The Foundation Stage: a survey of 144 Settings.* Ofsted

Paechter, C (1998) *Educating the Other: gender, power and schooling.* London: Falmer Press

Paechter, C (2001) Using poststructuralist ideas in gender theory and research. In B.Francis and C.Skelton (Eds.) *Investigating gender: contemporary perspectives in education.* Buckingham: Open University Press

Paechter, C (2003) Masculinities and Femininities as Communities of Practice, *Women's Studies International Forum*, 26(1), 69-77

Paechter, C (2006) Masculine femininities/feminine masculinities: power, identities and gender. *Gender and Education* 18 (3) p250-270

Paechter, C (2007) *Being Boys, Being Girls: Learning masculinities and femininities.* Maidenhead: Open University Press

Paley, V (1981) *Wally's Stories.* Harvard: Harvard University Press

Pearce, S (2005) *You wouldn't understand: white teachers in multiethnic classrooms.* Stoke on Trent: Trentham

Piaget, J (1977) *The Development of Thought.* Viking Press

Purves, L (2005) Segregating the sexes. *Times*

Reay,D (2001) 'Spice girls', 'nice girls', and 'tomboys': gender discourses, girls' cultures and femininities in the primary classroom. *Gender and Education* 13(2)p153-66

Renold, E (2005) *Girls, Boys and Junior Sexualities.* Abingdon: RoutledgeFalmer

Ribbens, J and Edwards, R (eds) (1998) *Feminist Dilemmas in Qualitative Research.* London: Sage Publications

Rich, D (2003) Bang! Bang! Gun play and why children need it, *Early Education Journal* 41

Robinson, K and Jones Diaz, C (2006) *Diversity and Difference in Early Childhood Education.* Maidenhead: Open University Press

Rogoff, B (1990) *Apprenticeship in Thinking.* Oxford: Oxford University Press

Shain, F (2003) *The Schooling and Identity of Asian Girls.* Stoke on Trent: Trentham Books

Simons, H (1982) Conversation piece: the practice of interviewing in case study research. In R.McCormick (ed) *Calling Education to Account.* London: Heinemann

Skelton, C (2001) Typical Boys? Theorizing masculinity in educational settings. In B. Francis, and

REFERENCES

C. Skelton, (eds) *Investigating gender: contemporary perspectives in education.* Buckingham: Open University Press

Skelton, C (2001) *Schooling the Boys: Masculinities and Primary Education.* Buckingham: Open University Press

Stanley, L and Wise, S (1993) *Breaking Out Again: Feminist Ontology and Epistemology.* London: Routledge

Swain, J (2003) How young schoolboys become somebody: the role of the body in the construction of masculinity, *British Journal of Sociology of Education* 24(3) p299-314

Thorne, B (1993) *Gender Play: Girls and boys in school.* Buckingham: Open University Press

Trevarthen, C (1998) The child's need to learn a culture. In M.Woodhead, D. Faulkner, and K. Littleton (eds) *Cultural Worlds of Early Childhood.* London: Routledge

Troyna, B and Hatcher, R (1992) *Racism in Children's Lives: A Study of mainly-White Primary Schools.* London: Routledge

Vygotsky, L (1978) *Mind in Society.* Harvard: Harvard Press

Walkerdine, V(1988) *The Mastery of Reason.* London: Routledge

Walkerdine, V and The Girls and Mathematics Unit (1989) *Counting Girls Out.* London: Virago

Walkerdine, V (1990) *Schoolgirl Fictions.* London: Verso Books

Walkerdine, V (1999) Violent boys and precocious girls: Regulating childhood at the end of the millennium. *Contemporary Issues in Early Childhood,* 1(1) p3-23

Walkerdine, V (2004) Developmental psychology and the study of childhood. In M.J. Kehily (ed) *An Introduction to Childhood Studies.* Oxford: Oxford University Press

Walkerdine, V, Lucey, H, and Melody, J (2001) *Growing Up Girl: Psycho-social Explorations of Gender and Class.* Basingstoke: Palgrave

Weedon, C (1987) *Feminist Practice and Poststructuralist Theory.* Oxford: Basil Blackwell

Weedon, C (1999) *Feminism, theory and the politics of difference.* Oxford: Blackwell Publishers

Wenger, E. (1998) *Communities of Practice: Learning, meaning and identity.* Cambridge: Cambridge University Press

Willis, P. and Trondman, M. (2000) Manifesto for Ethnography, *Ethnography* Vol 1 p5-16

Index

kiss chase 112

Lather, P. 1
legitimate peripheral
  participation
  definition 22
  in adult communities of
    practice 67
  in football 58-60
  in Nursery play 24, 61
  in same-sex activities 89
  in skipping 47, 53

lunchtime play 62, 72

MacNaughton, G. Xiii, xvi, 5,
  41, 121, 131
masculinity
  dominant 73
  nursery practices 26, 31,
    33, 72, 98, 99
  see also hegemonic
    masculinity

Ofsted xi, 39

Paechter, C. 23, 25, 26, 29,
  70, 72
Panoptic surveillance 70
participant observation 9
Piaget, J. 40, 41
pink
  as a marker of femininity
    68, 79
  as a pollutant for boys 74,
    106, 107, 108, 131
  as a symbol of girl power
    109, 110
play spaces 23, 26-29, 53,
  81, 96, 96-99, 113
  skipping and football 45,
    62
pleasure 62, 106, 116
  spirals of pleasure xix, 95,
    103, 105
policing gender borders 53,
  71, 79, 80, 107

power
  and knowledge xvii, xviii,
    6, 43
  and resistance xix
  between boys and girls
    34, 105
  between researcher and
    research participants 16-
    18
  in children's play episodes
    xiii, xix, 57, 95, 103, 105,
    112

race and ethnicity 75-78
  and identity xviii, 54, 69,
    76-78, 130
  definition xvii
reflexivity 7, 8
reification 46, 137
Renold, E. 52
research
  child participants 3
  context 2
  methods 1-19
  process, ethical and moral
    dilemmas 8, 15-18
researcher
  as adult 13, 105
roleplay 36, 93-100, 106, 107,
  114-116

self-surveillance xviii, 70
sexualities 52
  see also heterosexuality
skipping 47-50, 61, 104
  skipping rhymes 50
socio-dramatic play 29, 35-
  37, 93, 95, 106
spaces
  and power 43
  gendered use of 27, 28,
    95-98
  see also play spaces
staff
  in research 3
  reinforcing gender dualism
    38, 63, 83, 84-90
superhero play 72, 100, 128-
  130
  and girls 116

Thorne, B. 13, 108, 120, 131

Walkerdine, V. xvi, 41
water tray 30, 36, 106